Henry VIII's Motorcycle
or
A Tale of Two Trumpets

Also by Robert Barclay

Non-fiction
    The Art of the Trumpet-maker
    The Preservation and Use of Historic Musical Instruments
    Making a Natural Trumpet (with M. Münkwitz and R. Seraphinoff)

Fiction
    Triple Take: A Museum Story
    Death at the Podium
    Ask Me About My Bombshells
    Jacob the Trumpeter
    His Majesty's Grand Conceit

Publisher's note: In my view this author uses single quotes a great deal too often. He explains that this is because a number of the nouns specific to his theme have been employed with liberal interpretation as to their meaning. Highjacked was the word he used. I have instructed my editorial staff to comply with his wishes and have left them in place. The author also states that, to give his critics something to chew on, he has larded the text with a few errors. He won't tell me where they are.

Cover art: Loose Cannon Designs
Copy edit: A Good Idea Publications

Henry VIII's Motorcycle
or
A Tale of Two Trumpets

Robert Barclay

Library and Archives Canada Cataloguing in Publication

Title: Henry VIII's motorcycle, or, A tale of two trumpets / Robert Barclay.
Other titles: Henry VIII's motorcycle | Tale of two trumpets
Names: Barclay, R. L., author.
Identifiers: Canadiana 20210099909 | ISBN 9781988657226 (softcover)
Subjects: LCSH: Trumpet—Construction. | LCSH: Trumpet.
Classification: LCC ML961 .B244 2021 | DDC 788.9/21923—dc23

Copyright © 2021 Robert Barclay

All rights reserved. Except for use in any review or critical article, the reproduction or use of this work, in whole or in part, in any form by any electronic, mechanical or other means—including xerography, photocopying, scanning and recording—or in any information or storage retrieval system, is forbidden without express permission of the publisher

Published by
Loose Cannon Press

www.loosecannonpress.com

Table of Contents

Dedication	....	vi
Acknowledgements	....	vi
Preamble	....	vii
1. This One's All About Me	....	1
2. How One Became Two	....	7
3. The Invention of a Tradition	......	11
4. Circling the Wagons	....	15
5. Traditional Craftsmanship	....	21
6. Teaching Others	....	26
7. Copying and Reproduction	....	32
8. Getting Inside the Tradition	....	41
9. Henry VIII's Motorcycle	....	46
10. So, Now What?	....	49
Postamble	....	55
Feedback	....	60

Dedications

Around the time I discovered what was really going on with trumpets in the baroque orchestra, I happily encountered a small cadre of metalworkers, scholars and trumpeters who practiced fullhearted support for the instrument played during the 17th and 18th centuries. This book is dedicated to those unwavering individuals, who have been an inspiration to me over many years. Although I would like to name each of them, I fear omissions, but I feel sure they all know of whom I speak.

One particular individual does deserve special mention, though: the late Robert Oades, trumpeter and professor at the University of Ottawa, who was ever a steady supporter of my work and my ideas.

Acknowledgements

I would like to thank all those kind people who read and commented on the various drafts of this *minimum opus*. Louise Bacon, Crispian Steele-Perkins, Richard Seraphinoff, Matthew Parker, Sabine Klaus, Friedemann Immer and Michael Wright all contributed greatly in guiding my simplistic handling of several very complex and contentious issues. Nevertheless, all expressions, statements, criticisms and conclusions may be laid entirely at my charge, for I am brazed to 't.

Preamble

> 'You all remember,' said the Controller, in his strong deep voice, 'you all remember, I suppose, that beautiful and inspired saying of Our Ford's: "History is bunk." History,' he repeated slowly, 'is bunk.'
>
> Aldous Huxley, *Brave New World*

I hope you didn't buy this little book because you were beguiled by the cover. If you're really into alternative history, the idea of the Tudor king hurtling around the grounds of Hampton Court Palace on a motorcycle might have been quite appealing. Well, sorry to disappoint you, but Henry VIII remains steadfastly a horseman, although in this narrative Clio the Muse of History herself is taken for a ride. The subtitle—*A Tale of Two Trumpets*—is what the book is really all about, but I was so taken with the cover art that I couldn't resist the subterfuge. But, even if you know very little about what goes on in the modern baroque orchestra, read on and you'll be exposed to one of the longest running confidence tricks in history, 60 years and counting. That little fact alone should intrigue you, and perhaps recompense somewhat for having bought this book under false pretenses.

On the other hand, if you're a baroque music afficionado, cracking the spine of this book will serve you well. There's a lot of information on the many aspects of the recreation and use of historic musical instruments. In addition, you will learn how one trumpet became two, how authenticity bowed to expediency, and how the international cover-up of sharp practice continues to this day. More than this, you will learn how beautiful the baroque trumpet is when played in its rightful milieu.

There is no better tract on the subject.

Of course, you might be one of the baroque trumpet folks who know all about this stuff anyway, and are sick of hearing about it. Especially sick of me prosing on. Well, you're reading this right now, so there's surely some vested interest in your continuing. You might be amused, intrigued, annoyed or even (who knows?) informed, all of which are the elicited emotional outcomes of being exposed to great writing. Mind you, my kind of wisdom might be the one usually associated with the pain of impacted teeth.

You decide…

Chapter One
This One's All About Me

> Never be afraid to make a fool of yourself.
> Christopher Plummer

All right Your Majesty; kick-start your bike and let's get this narrative on the road. After publishing a great deal of technical stuff over many years, I got a hankering for historical fiction.[1] A few novels later, it occurred to me that the greatest piece of historical fiction was staring me right in the face all along, hence this work on the baroque trumpets… both of them. Will you continue reading if I promise that this little book will be the last thing I'll ever write on the subject?

I have been enthusiastic about the natural trumpet for the greater part of my life, and have made a large number of them over many years. I am no expert in playing the instrument and have never professed otherwise. I like to hide my slight ability in an ensemble of a dozen or so other players more talented than me. The most common charge levelled against me when I write something that others don't like, is that I have no right to criticize their practices if I am not, myself, a practitioner. This is, of course, comprehensive bollocks. Though I am not an orthopedic surgeon, if one of their number were to botch an operation on my knee, I would bloody well criticize. No, I might not be an expert kneesiologist, but I could sure as hell tell them what they had done wrong. I can equally praise them for a job well done, of course, which I do from firsthand experience. The issue of critical comment is as common for knees as it is for trumpets.

There is one important issue I need to raise before you read any further. During my entire instrument-making career I have had the unashamed luxury of a well-paid, full-time, pension-indexed government job. Making instruments according to historical principles, and offering them for sale, is easy when you don't have to worry where the next few dollars are coming from. I do respect and appreciate the work of all those craftspeople out there who don't have the privilege of a soapbox to stand on and preach from. As a corollary, I have had the same privilege of listening to and criticizing the use and misuse of the trumpet of the baroque era from my high pulpit. I respect those players who go out every day, placing their skills on the line in public, being obliged to perform to the highest level for their sustenance. They use the tools they have to get the job done. Again, fine to criticize, but put yer money where yer mouth is.

I intend to.

Of key importance to the analysis that constitutes this book is that I am a *consumer* of the music not a producer. I am on the outside of the culture, but looking in. That's my critical slant. So, though I may be outside the business of laying down the notes professionally, I am intimately concerned with, and informed about, how it is done. And my lack of musical education and talent are offset by boundless enthusiasm, commitment and hard study.

I think this is a fairly solid set of qualifications for what follows.

Over a long career in the metalwork shop I have built nearly 100 natural trumpets. I hear from some quarters within our little community the odd mutter about the quality of my workmanship, but I stand by it and I am confident that I have done a fairly good job.[2] I could not have begun this work, or continued it to great critical acclaim, without a close working relationship with the players. (I deal with this in detail in Chapter Five, *Traditional Craftsmanship*.) I cite a cadre of French *trompettistes* who gave me harmonious feedback and advice in the formative stages of the craft, and also the many purchasers of my instruments over the years.

Then I credit my good friends and colleagues whose enthusiasm and energy launched an international trumpet-making workshop that prospered far beyond anyone's wildest dreams. (See Chapter Six, *Teaching Others*.) Also to be credited in no uncertain terms are the professional organizations that have lauded my attention to the natural trumpet, and presented me with their accolades.[3]

I began the production of natural trumpets, using sound historical principles, as an exercise in early technology. I wanted to explore the 17th and 18th century workshops in exactly the same way as the practitioners of early music; to visit the place where the tools were used and to emulate that use.[4] It would be very satisfying to revisit my 1992 book *The Art of the Trumpet-maker* and bring it up to date. After all, a great deal has happened in my understanding during the quarter of a century since it was published, and much research has been undertaken by those individuals I cited in the dedication to this book. However, there are others among the critics of that work who are much more qualified than me, so it's over to them. Although I may not have the greatest expertise, knowledge or experience, I like to write of what I know, and I enjoy doing it. In a long career of working with experts in many fields, I have often witnessed the tragedy of immense knowledge going to waste because the carrier is unable, or unwilling, to set it down in writing. So, to all of those who know a great deal more on the topic of the natural trumpet than I do, *write it down*. I'm happy to be left with a historical document that has my name on it, for better or for worse. I still earn royalties.

What began as an academic exercise in the late 1980s, with the intended outcome of a published work or two, made a segue into instrument production. It seemed that my experimental material proved to be very playable instruments in their natural form. I made 10 experiments of one sort and another before number 11 was judged by a French colleague as a working musical instrument. As very few makers at that time were producing instruments based on historical techniques, this enhanced playing facility was not lost on me. (I knew of the work of Ron Collier, Geert Jan van der Heide and the brothers Thein, but in no great detail.) I suspected at the time that there was a distinct link between playability and handwork. Trumpeter and scholar Don Smithers had alluded to as much in an article in *Scientific American* where he and his co-authors stated that old instruments played better in tune than modern facsimiles.[5]

I had absolutely no intention of turning my basement workshop into a trumpet factory. It was an accident. Honest, officer! But when you find that skilled musicians really like your products, make beautiful music on them, and urge you to make more, what would *you* do? Besides, my three eldest were going through university at the time, so my wife and I were able to reckon their school fees in a novel currency unit called the trumpets-worth. My first trumpets were modelled after Hanns Hainlein of 1632.[6] I made a drawing of the instrument, and to thank the custodian museum for kindness in granting permission, I donated the original to them.[7] The Hainlein trumpet certainly worked well and before I knew it, I was in production. I offered instruments in brass or sterling silver, sometimes with gold-plated fittings. Later I produced trumpets based on a 1746 instrument by Johann Leonard Ehe III, one of a set of three.[8] I had made a drawing of this one some years before and was very fortunate, with a grant awarded by the Canada Council for the Arts, to visit European collections with colleague Jean-François Madeuf for conducting assessments and selection of suitable examples. Of the many instruments in the collections we visited in a whirlwind tour of a week, the trumpets by Johann Leonard Ehe III scored the highest points.

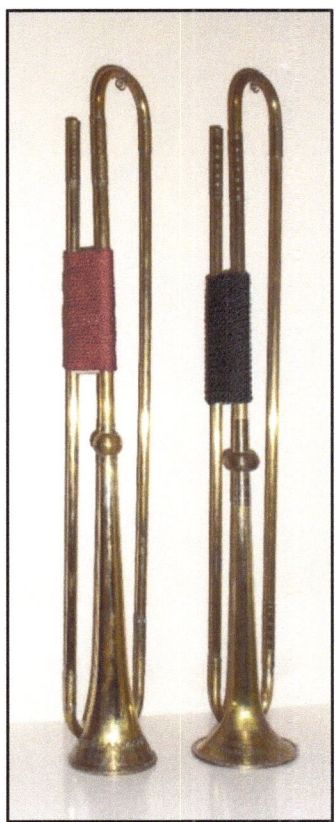

Figure 1: My Hainlein copy (left) and Ehe copy (right).

Before I settled down to making natural trumpets, I produced a few conjectural Renaissance slide-trumpets, an alto trombone, and a couple of portative organs. I made my final production trumpet a decade ago, and was pleased to engrave the garland with: I KORINTER 15:52. I gave a retirement announcement at a brass instrument conference in Basel and was delighted to be regaled with the toccata from Monteverdi's *Orfeo* by three of my French colleagues. I have made more brass instruments since but only for leisure and exploration, with the exception of one close copy (see Chapter Seven, *Copying and Reproduction*). Among the leisure instruments are a box trumpet, a walking stick trumpet, and diverse other anomalies of the brass instrument world.⁹

Figure 2 (left): The box trumpet taken apart to show how it's done.
Figure 3 (right): The walking stick trumpet with bell detached and ferrule and knob inserted. (Images courtesy of National Music Museum, The University of South Dakota, Mark Olencki, Photographer)

I have only ever made natural trumpets because I have always followed historical practices and prototypes, and I have adhered to this philosophy unswervingly. However, this little book deals with two kinds of instruments found in the present-day baroque orchestra: ones like mine that replicate the originals as closely as possible, and another kind developed from the 1960s onwards, where the vibrating air column is modified by the use of vents, or fingerholes. I'll discuss the development of these vented trumpets (as they are termed in this book) in detail in subsequent chapters because that's what my tale of two trumpets is all about.

Later on, I will have some words to say, from a consumer's point of view, along the lines *not* of what is used, but what is purveyed, what is projected, and what is sold as the real thing. If those chapters of the book are received with scorn and anger it's probably because those particular readers jump to conclusions before all the evidence is in. My advice to them is to read *all the words* right to the end. But know this: these words of mine won't make a damned bit of difference to current and future practice, any more than my article 'The Vented Trumpet: A New Species of Instrument' made any damned difference 20 years ago.[10] That's not why I wrote it then, and it's not why I'm writing this now. The tale of two trumpets extends into the foreseeable future, and this is an undeniable fact. This book is simply an exercise in setting the record straight in my own mind. It would be gratifying if it had some influence on the status quo, but I am not that naïve.

I look upon performances on the this newly-developed vented trumpet and the natural trumpet in same way I do my dining experiences; I'll zap some frozen fish fingers and fries and eat 'em in front of the TV, or I'll go out to a restaurant for a nice meal and a glass of wine. Each experience is satisfying and enjoyable in its own right.

Now let's have a look backwards and see how it all got this way.

Notes

[1] I have appended some blatant self-promotion on pages 57 and 58.

[2] I dabble in many things, but perform none of them to the highest achievable standard. While I have been called a Renaissance man, I much prefer the accolade Jack of all trades, master of none. I am actually envious of those who do but one thing, and do it really well.

[3] The Nicholas Bessaraboff Prize, the Anthony Baines Memorial Prize and the Christopher Monk Award. (I hid these references in an endnote because I don't want to blow my own trumpet; I do it but poorly.)

[4] Barclay, R., 'Preliminary Studies on Trumpet Making Techniques in 17th and 18th Century Nürnberg,' *Festschrift für John Henry van der Meer zu seinem fünfundsechzigsten Geburtstag*, H. Schneider, 1987; and Barclay, R., *The Art of the Trumpet-maker: The Materials, Tools and Techniques of the 17th and 18th Centuries in Nuremberg* (Oxford: Oxford University Press, Early Music Series 14, 1992)

[5] Smithers, D., Wogram, K. and Bowsher, J., "Playing the Baroque Trumpet,' *Scientific American*, 254:4 (1986), pp. 109-115.

[6] Stadtmuseum München, 67/95.

[7] Sadly, this was only verbal permission. Lacking a document in writing was a salutary lesson in covering your arse, which omission I repaired by active work on an international committee: Various Authors, *Recommendations for Regulating the Access to Musical Instruments in Public Collections*, Comité international pour les musées et collections d'instruments de musique (CIMCIM) (1985)

[8] Germanisches Nationalmuseum, MIR 218.

[9] See Klaus, S., *Trumpets and Other High Brass* (Vermillion, S. Dakota: National Music Museum, 2012) pp. 182 and 231.

[10] Barclay, R., 'A New Species of Instrument: The Vented Trumpet in Context,' *Historic Brass Society Journal*, Vol. 10 (1998), pp. 1-13.

Chapter Two
How One Became Two

> They'll have me whipped for speaking true, thou'lt have me whipped for lying, and sometimes I am whipped for holding my peace. I had rather be any kind o' thing than a fool.
>
> William Shakespeare, *King Lear*

Applying handwork and no-nonsense authentic practice to making trumpets was spurred on by my disappointing discovery that the 'natural' trumpets featured on many recordings I owned were actually nothing of the sort, and that their purported antecedents bordered on historical fiction. It seemed to me axiomatic that reproduction of the music of the period would go in lockstep with reproduction of the instruments. This was so in the fine handwork of the baroque violin, the elegant lathe craftsmanship of the baroque oboe and flute, the intricate mechanical woodwork of the harpsichord. I have immersed myself in the workshops of a wide range of musical instrument craftsmen, and absorbed every aspect of them like a member of the phylum *Porifera*.[1] In the production of all these instruments I saw a fine and balanced harmony within and across craft and practice; a historical wholeness that placed practice of the music, and the tools to effect it, securely in their context.

The 'natural' trumpet shattered that harmony.

I discovered that the so-called 'natural' trumpets on my cherished CD recordings were made from spun cornet bells attached to lengths of seamless tubing, their bells insultingly graced with cast-off doorknobs. A series of fingerholes—or tone-holes, vents, call them what you will—allowed the small-bore modern mouthpiece in the tapered leadpipe to make the things play in tune in equal temperament (see Figure 8, p. 17). Their users called them 'nats,' which I found particularly odious. These, to my way of thinking, were a gross affront to all that was fine and cultured in my imagination of baroque music.

They were a cabbage fart in a vestry.

Before anybody gets their knickers in a twist, let me state right from the outset that I am not criticizing current practice in the manufacture and use of these instruments, at least not in musical terms; things have come a long way since these egregious examples were spawned. These days, many vented trumpets on offer are gorgeous examples of craftsmanship, finely finished and turned out with precision and great attention to detail. I am thinking particularly of a line of Swiss-made instruments, but more about that anon.

This book is not about the use of the vented trumpet in baroque music, but about how that use is portrayed. Over the years, a wide variety of trumpets have been used: the many kinds of valved instruments, ones equipped with various numbers and placement of vents, and natural single loops, more resembling their early antecedents. Most of them are legitimate in their own way, *provided your listeners know what dish they are being served*. Besides, where would we be if our appreciation of the music of any period was confined to a purist ethic that allowed no compromise? It's obvious that it doesn't matter a tinker's cuss what instrument is used to play the music of bygone times. I have some wonderful 33-rpm vinyls: for example, John Wilbraham playing baroque trumpet concertos;[2] and how could one fault William Lang in 'The Trumpet Shall Sound?'[3] They make lovely music on their valved trumpets. I would no more criticize these instrumental choices than I would Glenn Gould or Angela Hewitt for playing Bach on the grand piano. And in the realm of vented trumpets, I cannot think of a finer rendition of the trumpet part to Handel's *Eternal Source of Light Divine* than that played by Crispian Steele-Perkins.[4] Or what of Dennis Ferry's accompaniment to Scarlatti's *Si suoni la tromba*?[5] Gorgeous music brought to us by practitioners at the very pinnacle of their craft.

I repeat: it's not about the instrument; it's about the sales job.

Let's have a look at what happened in the creation of those 'natural' trumpets—which they weren't—and which were later rebranded as 'baroque' trumpets, which they weren't either. I recall with fondness an observation I made 20 years ago in the question period of a presentation on the subject of the natural trumpet at a Historic Brass Society[6] conference: 'You refer to the widespread use of the natural trumpet... but I don't know who these players are. Unless, of course, you are confusing the natural trumpet with the natural trumpet.' This was met with puzzlement, so I continued: 'To clarify, perhaps you are lumping the "natural trumpet" and the natural trumpet together into a single category?' I remember adding the air quotes with my index fingers in the clarification, although I was afterwards admonished for being reckless and making a nuisance of myself. I thought it was a good question then, and I still think it is. As to being a nuisance, I paraphrase Arthur Dent 'I ask merely for information.'[7]

I could pose the same question today as I did a couple of decades back: 'You refer to the widespread use of the baroque trumpet... but I don't know who these players are. Unless, of course, you are confusing the "baroque trumpet" with the baroque trumpet.' Happily, I *do* know who these players are. There are many more people playing the trumpet used in the baroque period now than there were 20 years ago. But that's another thread entirely.

If you're not inside the modern baroque trumpet world, you might have found the foregoing discussion confusing. At this stage, let's just say that there is clearly some subterfuge at work here...

All this as a prelude to a discussion on taxonomy. Some readers of this little tract will know exactly what I'm talking about, but there may be some who are unaware of these two kinds of trumpet used in baroque music (aside from the good old valves, of course). I hope the former will indulge the latter in getting us all up to speed. So, here's how I'll clarify the issue of terminology throughout this book:

- Natural trumpet: the real baroque trumpet; the valve-less instrument of the 17th and 18th centuries
- Vented trumpet: the 'baroque' trumpet with tone- or finger-holes introduced in the later 20th century
- Valve trumpet: the modern chromatic instrument equipped with valves devised at the beginning of the 19th century

Brass instruments produce the notes of the natural harmonic scale, and over their history various systems have been applied to expand this limited range by modifying the resonating length while playing, including valves, keys and slides. The natural trumpet is an instrument that has no modifying devices, and thus is capable of producing only the notes of the natural harmonic series in which it is pitched.[8] Instruments in the keys of C and D were most common during the baroque period, although preserved examples show a wide range from B-flat at the lowest to F at the high end. The tuning specific to the time and place of the instrument's manufacture and use must be taken into account when assigning pitch. Crooks and tuning bits were used to change keys and to fine-tune. Natural trumpets are in nominally eight-foot pitch, thus giving at least 16 available notes.

Figure 4. The harmonic series in C. Every article on brass instruments has to include one of these; it's almost obligatory. (This is known as the baroque two-hole system.[9])

The ratio of cylindrical tubing to tapered or flared tubing gives a tuning based upon the standard Western primary intervals of octave and fifth. Notably, several notes do not fall on the scale of western music, especially in the modern system of equal temperament. The 11th harmonic is a quarter tone between what we consider to be F and F#, the 13th is flat, and the 7th and 14th are also flat, but less so. The reader should note that the diagram on the previous page, and the text that accompanies it, are mere adumbrations presented purely for heuristic reasons. When applied to brass instruments in the real world, it is never as simple; these definitions break down and discordant opinions ensue. (I wouldn't have put the blasted diagram in, but everybody else does.)

When played alone as a military signaling instrument, or in an ensemble with other trumpets and added drums, this scale is not problematic. However, from the early 17th century onwards when the trumpet began to be scored with other instruments in what would become the orchestra—such as strings and woodwinds—trumpet players needed to temper these awkward tones, and particularly to play the 11th harmonic as either F or F#.

I have alluded the fact that, during the second half of the 20th century, playing the trumpet with other instruments in baroque music was made easier through a series of experiments that resulted in the vented trumpet. As I mentioned in the previous chapter, because of its taxonomical difference to the trumpet of the baroque period, I have suggested that the vented trumpet be classified as a new species of instrument. Its social history and technical development are dealt with later. A systematic description of this 'unnatural trumpet,' which I can highly recommend, has been published by trumpet player, scholar and instrument-maker Graham Nicholson.[10]

In view of this creative adaptation, it is not accurate to refer to a 'revival' of this particular instrument, as several authors do.[11] What we have here is a confusion between revival and invention, which is curious in the face of a wealth of encouragement to describe the situation accurately. There is vagueness over what is a very clear taxonomic distinction. The baroque trumpet *revival* has indeed happened, but it has nothing to do with vents, or toneholes, or finger-holes, and everything to do with playing the instrument for which the music was written. The trumpet of the baroque is now making a true revival at the hands (and embouchures) of a few dedicated specialists and their students. This involves the developing and refinement of the original instrumental resources, and rediscovering the art of playing the natural trumpet in concert with other instruments; a quite distinct musical accomplishment having nothing to do with mechanical compromise.

Thus, the current situation has arisen where two discrete kinds of instrument may be encountered in recordings and concerts of baroque music, with the majority of listeners ignorant of which is which. The vented trumpet is, in fact, the sole instrument of the baroque orchestra that has no historical counterpart in that era.

In the following chapters I'll look at some of the reasons behind this fascinating bifurcation, and discuss just how a tradition can be invented.

Notes

[1] For example, I had an active role in the musical instrument exhibition *Opus* at the Canadian Museum of Civilization. See Begin, C., *Opus: the making of musical instruments in Canada* (Ottawa: Canadian Museum of Civilization, 1992)

[2] *Baroque Trumpet Concertos*, Argo ZRG 585 (1969)

[3] *Messiah*, Philips 802 721/AY (1966)

[4] *Music for Royal Occasions*, Hyperion CDA 66315 (1984)

[5] *Scarlatti–Melani*, Harmonia Mundi HM 5137 (1984)

[6] Interestingly, the Historic Brass Society entertains the users of this bogus equipment, an argument for an extremely flexible definition of the term 'historic.' There is nothing about the instruments that is historic, save for the fact that their invention dates back to the 1960s, so I guess this would be enough justification for cheese-paring literalists.

[7] Adams, D., *Life, the Universe and Everything* (London and Sydney: Pan Books, 1982), p. 13.

[8] Von Hornbostel, E.M. and Sachs, K., *Classification of Musical Instruments*, trans. A. Baines and K.P. Wachsmann, *Galpin Society Journal*, 14 (1961), pp. 3-12.

[9] You place your lips against the little hole, and the sound comes out of the bigger one at the other end. And if you play like me, it's God-awful.

[10] Nicholson, G., 'The Unnatural Trumpet,' *Early Music*, Vol. xxxviii, No. 2 (2010), pp. 193-202.

[11] Foster, J., *The Baroque Trumpet Revival* (Chandler, Arizona: Hickman Music Editions, 2015); *op cit* Klaus, (2012) pp. 249-59.

Chapter Three
The Invention of a Tradition

> Invented a vent, a vent, a vent;
> Invented a vent, a vent, a vent.
> Invented a vent!
> Invented a vent!
> Invented a, vented a vent.
>
> Kurt Vonnegut, *The Sirens of Titan*
> (var. with apologies)

I have found it fascinating and intellectually satisfying to have been privileged, over a period of decades, to watch a tradition being invented before my very eyes. Tradition—the handed-down way of doing things—is a very flexible concept. What sometimes appears as a long-standing and unquestioned practice can, on analysis, be found to be more recent than supposed and far more philosophically fragile. Institutions, in particular, can be dressed by political expediency to possess ancient but quite spurious antecedents.[1] Among many examples are the eisteddfod of Wales and the tartans of Scotland, both invented traditions created by a drive for identity within distinct cultures absorbed into Great Britain. The classic and unquestioned view of the American Wild West is another enduring mythology, one created by the film industry and mass-marketed until it became 'true.'

Now it's time to take a look at the tale of two trumpets from a social perspective, examining not what the instrument now is, but how its tradition was invented. (I know you're thirsting for Henry VIII and his motorcycle, but you'll just have to wait a bit. I'm sorry, but you can always skip the stuff in between and go straight to Henry VIII's ninth chapter if you want.) Anyhow, this newly-invented trumpet with tone-holes badly needed a backstory. In order to invent a tradition, you need supporting documentation and some systematic social engineering. People must be led to believe the mythology; concert-goers must not question the appearance or the playing technique of those authentic trumpets. There is much wool to be pulled over many eyes. With the rise in conspiracy theories in the present decade, we have seen how laughably easy it is to create an alternative truth—people can clearly be led to believe *anything*—and things were really no different when the vented trumpet was being launched.[2]

Here's how it was done.

The instrument of the baroque period was always a problem. In the first half of the 20th century, when early music began to be examined in a historical context outside a well-established canon of practice, the trumpet just couldn't be made to behave. The reliance upon only the notes of the natural harmonic series was crippling. A few players did make successful experiments on original instruments over a hundred years ago, but few dared to do so in public. J. S. Bach was regarded as the exemplar of writing for the instrument of the period, but just how the notes were extracted remained an intriguing mystery. The century-long story of the Bach trumpet makes fascinating reading, although it is redundant in the framework of this book, and likely beyond my ability to do it justice anyway.

Then something exciting happened: the discovery, published in 1961, of a trumpet by Johann Gottfried Haltenhof of Hanau with a nodal tone-hole about halfway along its length. A ragged mess of a hole it was, but a hole nonetheless. Opening this hole with a finger would remove all the odd numbered harmonics—the ones that have a nodal point at this place in the bore—thus increasing the space between the even ones. This discovery was eventful; it caused a profound change of direction in the search for Bach's instrument, while setting development on a false path that has diverged ever since.[3]

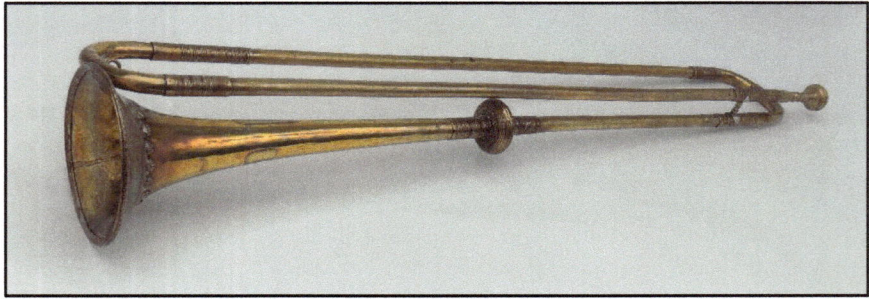

Figure 5: The Johann Gottfried Haltenhof trumpet of 1790. (Image courtesy of Historisches Museum Frankfurt.)

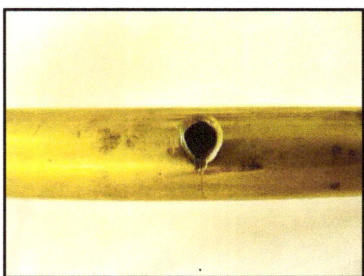

Figure 6: The tone hole on the Haltenhof trumpet. It might be a bit hard on the finger. If some late-18th century trumpeter had asked me to do this, I think I would have smoothed off the edges a bit, and maybe soldered a chimney on. (Image courtesy of Sabine Klaus.)

The description of this instrument was seized upon as the answer to the mystery. I am reminded of the 1912 'discovery' by Charles Dawson of skull fragments at Piltdown in Sussex. Here was very clearly the 'missing link,' a skull with both humanoid and simian characteristics; exactly the piece of the puzzle that savants had been seeking ever since Darwin had shown us that we were, indeed, descended from apes! Strange how these discoveries arise just when they are most needed, but hardly surprising that they are taken up with such alacrity. It seems that discrimination takes a back seat under these circumstances. (It was not until 1953 that the remains of Piltdown Man were shown to be bogus.[4]) In the social context of the mid-20th century, it is not difficult to see why the Haltenhof discovery was adopted so avidly. The supposed 'tone-hole' in the instrument was seen as the culmination of a century of speculation, and showed a practical way forward.[5] The instrument was made in 1790 and the aftermarket adaptation could have been done at any time after that, of course. It was thus far too late for having anything to do with playing the baroque trumpet. Nevertheless, and in spite of the instrument's late date and the clear crudeness of the adaptation, here was the evidence that was so desperately needed.

Following this discovery, instrument makers jumped in with both feet, producing trumpets with one nodal hole, and then two, that would help correct the 'out of tune' harmonics, and another that, when opened, could provide a whole range of harmonics four or five steps higher. The well-known portrait by Hausmann of Gottfried Reiche, Bach's trumpeter in Leipzig, holding a coiled instrument was enlisted for the cause. On a coiled instrument you could distribute the holes along the bore so they could be covered by the fingers of one hand! You can't see them in the Hausmann portrait, but let's not worry about that. Thus, the 'clarino' was born with all the suitable historical antecedents to back up its authenticity. But it still needed solid validation.

Among many examples, the cementing of this invented tradition is very well illustrated in the series of vinyl recordings produced under the Archiv label by Deutsche Grammophon. There are strong positivistic elements in the producers' approach, the aim being to present the work *wie es eigentlich gewesen* (as it really was) but with a catastrophic failure in the trumpet section, as I will show. The Archiv record sleeves include fold-out spreads or booklets describing the works in music-historical terms. The documents are organized in groups of *Forschungsberich* (research fields) and are set out in fine and dense academic type. Instrumentation is described systematically; many of the string instruments used are original to the period and their dates are cited lovingly. An example of this systematic approach, which is most relevant to this discussion, is the trumpets used in F. W. Zachow's *Vom Himmel kam der Engel Schar*. They are described as: '*Helmut Finke, Herford, 1961; Rekonstruktionen von Otto Steinkopf nach dem Porträt des Trompeters Gottfried Reiche.*'[6] A reader lacking a deep understanding of this particular instrumentation would naturally take this statement at face value and assume a quite undeserved 'authenticity' in the recording, especially when it appears in such a scholarly setting. (Indeed, I did when I bought the record almost 50 years ago. It was only later that I saw a picture of the instrument.) However, these seemingly solid academic credentials are built upon faery dust and moonshine. The Steinkopf 'reconstructions,' with their Finke-holes, are based upon a painting of an instrument that has no extant counterpart, together with a further assumption of the existence of tone-holes on this imaginary instrument. If one of my students produced an academic thesis based upon such premises, I would feed it into the shredder and tell him or her to come back with something worth defending, even if it was couched in the best academese and formatted luxuriously.[7]

If this bogus academic con job was not enough, we discover that this trumpet has a bell form unlike any on an instrument of the baroque period, and specifically nothing like the one in the Reiche portrait. In fact, it looks just like an off-the-shelf bell of a short, high-pitched piccolo trumpet. Coincidence, doubtless. Naturally, the tone colour of this concoction is far removed from anything coming out of the bell of an 18th century instrument. So, what we have here is, at best, conjectural, while being musically and practically an entirely different instrument from that scored for by Bach. It is yet another iteration in the centuries-long quest for Bach's trumpet, but takes the exploration further away from, not nearer to, the goal.

So, with the vented trumpet now established in the modern baroque orchestra, a tradition had been invented. Isn't it fascinating that the radical 1960s-style break from tradition—overturning the classical canons and starting afresh—has now turned full circle and there exists another fully entrenched canon of practice?

A 'new' tradition.

Plus ça change, plus c'est la même chose.

Notes

[1] Hobsbawm, E. and Ranger, T. eds., *The Invention of Tradition* (Cambridge: Cambridge University Press, 1983).
[2] You would love my chapter on the Bottle Conjuror in *His Majesty's Grand Conceit*.
[3] Kirchmeyer, H., 'Die Rekonstruktion der "Bachtrompete",' *Neue Zeitschrift für Musik*, 122 (1961), pp. 13-45.
[4] In contrast, the vented trumpet was clearly bogus as soon as it was unearthed.
[5] The harmonic trumpet of 1787 by William Shaw of London was also cited, although it also was made long after the baroque era.
[6] *Advent und Weinachten im alten Halle und Leipzig*, Deutsche Grammophon, Archiv, 198327 (1963).
[7] Trumpet-maker and player Graham Nicholson had made great advances in creating a model of a coiled trumpet like the one Reiche is shown holding, a recreation of the instrument well worth defending.

Chapter Four
Circling the Wagons

The maestro says it's Mozart
But it sounds like bubblegum.
Leonard Cohen, *Waiting for the Miracle*

An instrument for circumventing performance problems has now been invented. This is nothing new, of course; throughout the history of their craft, instrument-makers have been reacting to satisfy changing musical demands. The requirements of composers and players create a dynamic triad with the makers, pushing development forward in a mutually rewarding fashion. Musical instrument museums and collection curators have great fondness for illustrating the 'evolution' of items in their collections.[1] For example, the bell form of the trumpet shows a gradual increase in flare and a narrowing of the throat through the 17th century. And the sudden proliferation of valved inventions in the early 19th century needs no further discourse. Development of musical instruments in form and function is normal.

There is one powerful difference when it comes to the vented trumpet: the invention seems to be a bit of an embarrassment. The normal reaction of the musical instrument-maker in lauding his product is absent here. Instead, the development is slipped into the baroque music culture sideways, as it were, in the hope that those on the outside will not be aware of it, while those on the inside can carry on as if nothing had happened. Naturally, musical instrument catalogues advertise these perforated wares, but those are hardly directed at the public. Instead, the music producers' quasi-academic treatment has beguiled the everyday reader and listener into a false sense of confidence. In effect, we have here an intellectual smokescreen, disingenuous if you are forgiving, but actually deliberately falsifying.

Where does the buyer stand in the face of this action? Legally speaking, such a misrepresentation would amount to fraud if it were perpetrated to make money. When I first became aware of it—and many more instances too numerous to detail—I wondered idly what recourse one would have under law. After all, I had parted with cash under a false assumption. Would it be possible to sue for a misleading description of a product? After all, with the Archiv label, Deutsche Grammophon was selling a product under false pretenses, as were many other record labels. This speculation is beyond naïve, of course, because the burden of proof would be elusive, but it was the natural reaction of one who felt cheated. I once asked a player of the vented trumpet what he thought of the potential for such claims: 'Oh, if I was charged with it, I'd just tell 'em I had all the holes closed.' (You even get a supply of rubber corks or screws with some instruments.) That's the kind of argument that could be used in any legal challenge. Laughed out of court, it would be.

It would, therefore, be unwise to refer to fraud in this little book—just in case any reader gets the wrong idea—so let's use a nice gentle word like hoax instead. The Oxford English Dictionary defines a hoax as: 'A humorous or mischievous deception with which the credulity of the victim is imposed upon.' This way we can all pretend the misrepresentation of the natural trumpet to the public at large is all just a bit of harmless fun, can't we?

But what is the exact nature of the chain of culpability here? Who is responsible for creating this 'alternate truth?' I possess no evidence that the inventers and the musicians had any complicity in any of these sales schemes. After all, they are in the maw of a great machine that churns out consumable product, and who knows how many desks the information passes over, or what decisions are taken on the way from artist to printed text? But, for sure, there is equally no evidence that they provided honest copy, or took pains to disabuse the copywriters of this false narrative. This seems to me to be, at least, culpability by association.

From Deutsche Grammophon's vinyls onward it became a characteristic of recordings of early music to include booklets featuring lists of the instruments used, with details of dates, makers and other information considered persuasive. It is not unusual to see the trumpets in these recordings described in terms of the models upon which they were based, even though no mention is made of systems of venting and other critical details of construction. One can do this by such subterfuges as '*after* Johann Leonhard Ehe' or '*based on* a model by Wolf Wilhelm Haas.' The trumpet shall sound, but far from incorruptible. When I was a little boy, my mum told me that this was 'telling porkies.'[2] I did find one ray of probity over my years of buying CDs, though. The liner notes of Friedemann Immer's *Balleti: Sonaten, Serenaden am Hof am Kremsier* mention the use of ventholes and state that, 'These tones of the natural harmonic series sound unpleasant to our modern ears.'[3] Fair enough. Now, how hard was that?

Now to the actual vented trumpet itself. There have been many systems of vents introduced over the years, from a single one situated on the back bow, through to full sets of four, resulting in an absence of any unmodified notes among the upper harmonics. In Continental practice the vents were placed on a second rear bow—creating a double coil at the rear—while in English usage the holes were placed around the middle of the lower yard, thus maintaining a passing visual resemblance to the real thing. Fingering schemes vary a great deal, depending upon the model and system used, and also on the particular preferences of the player, mouthpiece choice, etc.

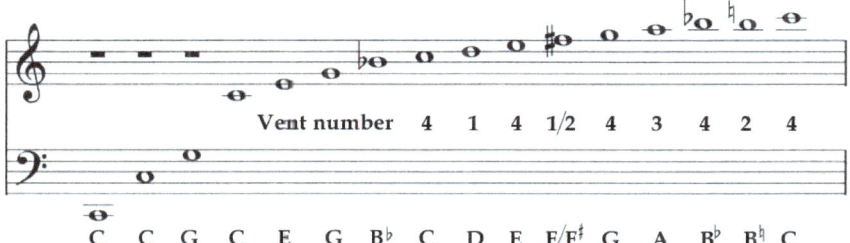

Figure 7: One of several systems for a four-hole vented trumpet, modified from various schemes published on the Web, and presented for heuristic reasons only. (Compare this with the baroque two-hole system shown in Figure 4.)

As I mentioned earlier, as a craftsman I was justifiably appalled at the idea of throwing found components together, which is how the first 'nats' were born. However, craftsmanship has come a long way since then. Although I have always had harsh things to say about those ugly early iterations—or experiments—and upon the necessity in the first place of using them in preference to the real thing, there is no doubt that metal instrument craftsmanship has risen to the challenge. With a natural trumpet one changes the key and adjusts the pitch with crooks and tuning bits. This simple expedient won't work with a vented instrument, because merely changing the length of the vibrating air column will throw out the tuning of the vents.

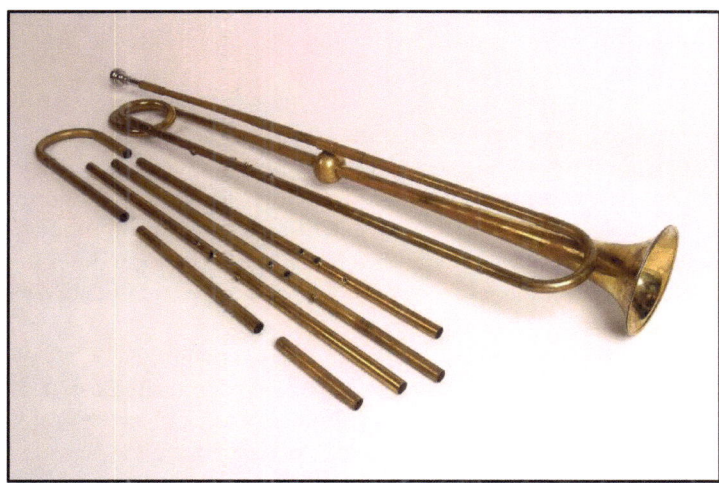

Figure 8: A typical vented trumpet of the English system with lower yards that can be substituted for different orchestral pitches. This is a wonderful example of applied musical engineering. (Alamy Stock Images)

Thus, for each orchestral pitch (e.g., A=415Hz, A=430Hz, or the modern standard of A=440Hz), a separate lower yard or back bow with vents is required. This results in a system of dismounting of components quite different from the original method of construction (see Chapter Five, *Traditional Craftsmanship*) and, of course, involves a whole mess of extra bits and pieces.

In point of fact, as I have said earlier, the intricacy and inventiveness of the trumpet with a venting system is to be praised not derided, although the illustration on the previous page shows the nuttiness that has resulted from contradictory decisions to 'keep it simple.' Compare this apparatus with the two trumpets shown in Figure 1. And let's not even contemplate anything but equal temperament! Any music director who would insist that players use this mass of plumbing has very clearly lost the plot. But choices have to be made and nobody said it was easy. Wouldn't it be so much better if music wasn't made by human beings…

The vented trumpet illustrated on the previous page is a touchingly ugly example of the old school, and it is true to say that brass instrument-making has improved greatly since this picture was taken. Nowadays, some makers are hand-forming their components, reflecting the historical approach to early music in the application of traditional techniques. Handwork represents a departure from the industrial-based systems of manufacture and that, at least, is one saving grace of this absurd industry. And in the ideal scenario (which only occurs in my dreams) instrument-makers will eventually have to abandon these contraptions and come back to the production of simple, well-proportioned historic instruments. In Chapter Ten I'll discuss why this isn't going to happen any time soon.

The question I had posed at that Historic Brass Society conference, mentioned earlier, highlighted what I saw as a deliberate obfuscation of the term 'natural trumpet.' In any event, the invented vent convention eventually prevented the term 'natural' being used with a straight face, so it was rebranded as the 'baroque trumpet.' Finally, after several decades of equivocal description, the trumpet-playing community generally settled on this term as being descriptive of the instrument when used in its modern context.

This is not a description of the instrument, though, is it? Whoever first decided on naming the instrument forgot to do a search to check if the name had already been taken. It had. When I write a book, I always run a check to make sure that somebody hasn't got my title already, and if they have, I need to think of something else. So, did these name-givers think that a term that was already in use could be appropriated without causing confusion? Apparently. After all, they had been using 'natural trumpet' for years with cavalier disregard for its meaning, so why not? 'What's in a name?' asks Juliet. Well, actually, a great deal, because an object does not exist without a unique name.

Assigning a specific noun is the actualization of the object. But if my name's Bob and your name's Bob and his name's Bob and that's Bob leaning on the bar over there, we clearly need a modifier.

At this point in the discussion my critics will doubtless accuse me of mere epistemological hair-splitting. However, such a charge could only result from shallow thinking or—which is much more germane to this discussion—a reluctance to look more deeply into the issue for fear of exposing something undesirable.

The 'baroque' trumpet needs a modifier and it doesn't have one, and besides, applying any qualifier to the noun must inevitably raise suspicions among those on the *outside*. In referring to 'inside' and 'outside' I am defining distinct cultures.[4] The two regimens of playing the two baroque trumpets in their distinct orchestral settings are the result of quite separate and divergent patterns of behaviour, but only when viewed from within their own circles of activity. To a large extent the audience—outside—perceives no distinction between them. From the outside, there is no nuance; simply groups of musicians playing together. However, the intricate choices of temperament, tuning and instrumental resources have created two distinct cultures that show, externally, only superficial resemblance. But in both cultures a baroque flute is a baroque flute; a baroque oboe is a baroque oboe; a baroque violin is a baroque violin; but a baroque trumpet is a... well, what is it? For sure, in describing the *real* baroque trumpet, I could say 'the trumpet of the baroque,' or the 'natural trumpet' (except the latter term has been beaten unconscious and left in a ditch with its pockets rifled) but it's not incumbent on me to do so. The players of the real thing got there first.

Their noun has been stolen.

I feel tolerably certain that if a player showed up to a gig with a modern nickel-silver flute and called it a baroque flute, there would be more than just raised eyebrows. (It's quite bizarre when you think about it: the player of a silvery mass of industrial axles, springs and keys gets booted out of the band, while the player with a gig-bag full of fittings the like of which would be unheard of two centuries ago gets the nod from the man at the front with the stick. There's no accounting for it really, is there?)

What we are witnessing in this constructed confusion of nomenclature is an act of cultural appropriation, where a dominant culture has adopted the symbol of another. The result of this dual reality is that the people on the *inside* of the vented trumpet culture know what they mean, but they're leery of modifiers for fear of letting the cat out of the bag. The public does not possess the information necessary to realize that there's a cover-up going on here—to a large extent they are not even aware of the distinct cultures—and they're not likely to get that information. That's why the accurate taxonomic description 'vented trumpet' can *never* be used in public.

It's a confession.

And then, before you know it, a simple passive description among people on the inside makes a key change into an active policy of deceit. Deceit is not too strong a term to use for a campaign of reeducation, as the following examples will show. In one of the many video presentations available online, the obfuscation is perpetuated by introducing the vented instrument as 'the natural trumpet *or* the baroque trumpet' as if the two instruments were somehow congruent. That is clearly the intention, and it is mendacious. It is four minutes into this presentation that the holes are excused, *en passant* and with no great clarity, as it is not explained even then that no single note from B-flat on the staff upwards is played unmodified! The instrument is described as being a 'reproduction of the trumpet of the baroque era' which, in view of the tone holes, is highly misleading. In another popular video, a player spends a full six minutes and fifty seconds describing and demonstrating the music of J. S. Bach on a vented trumpet without *once* mentioning the holes. You can *see* the holes! You can watch the fingers move! But nary a word. This is the opposite of enlightenment.[5] This is a disgraceful and shameful presentation.

It is unconscionable to fool the public like this. But, not only is it ethically derelict to misdirect in this way, it is also a great disservice to those who play the trumpet of the baroque period honestly. It is a slap in the face. I find this really disheartening, and it's sad to see professionals with high profiles, who should know better, associating their names with such a shabby hoax. It does not become them and they are diminished by it.

However, my carping and whining aside, the vented trumpet is played most gorgeously on one of those videos, and I would so love to hear that particular performer play the natural instrument. And what a fantastic ambassador she would be for the trumpet of the baroque with her divine playing! Too much to hope for, I know, but perhaps there's a parallel universe where she is such a proponent?

Wish I lived there…

Notes

[1] The word evolution has been grossly overused recently. The word 'development' has almost fallen out of use, to be replaced with a term that specifies organic change over many generations. Yeah, I know, there he goes again…

[2] Cockney rhyming slang: pork pies = lies.

[3] '…*klingen diese Töne der Naturtonreihe fur unser heutigen Hörgewohnheiten unsauber.*' (MDG I. 3369, 1990)

[4] As culture is one of the most difficult words to define in the English language, I give it mere lip service. There's a dissertation to be written here. I would gladly supervise.

[5] A quick on-line search will find these videos, and many more. You don't need me to direct you when firsthand evidence is so easily available.

Chapter Five
Traditional Craftsmanship

> The type of work which modern technology is so successful in reducing or eliminating, is skillful, productive work of the human hands, in touch with real materials…
> E.F. Schumacher, *Small is Beautiful*

Here I'll move away from the distasteful subject of cover-ups and falsehoods, and segue into a discussion of the handicrafts. And these are not invented traditions; these have antecedents in millennia and tools and techniques of great antiquity. As I stated earlier, I am sure it was the sight of those ghastly 'nats,' even before my trumpet-making career began, that drove me toward metal instrument handwork and a study of the history of technology. The world of baroque music *must*, I thought, be able to offer something better than this. I recall a workshop in the 1990s in Amsterdam where somebody had a gig bag for sale. It had large zipped pockets on each side, and I observed that these were for the bricks, so when the bag and its 'nat' were hurled into the canal it would be sure to sink. Of course, there were other, much better made instruments available; the line of Meinl und Lauber products, among others, offered a modicum of good taste, but when played without holes they were apparently quite intractable. There was clearly much to do. This chapter will enlarge upon my observation earlier that instruments made using historic techniques have enhanced playing capabilities.

The relationships between a musical instrument, its player and the craftsperson who creates it are among the subtlest and most nuanced of all human interactions. An almost symbiotic relationship between instrument and musician has been characterized by a host of subjective elements related to feel and comfort, and even notions of anthropomorphism.[1] I have heard players state that a new instrument has to be 'taught' how to play well, and others who have held forth on the musical personalities of their instruments. It would be reckless of me to scorn these notions simply because no tangible proof is forthcoming. You yell 'bullshit' at your peril. None of these relationships between the user and the object lend themselves to systematic analysis, although much effort has been spent attempting to answer questions around the superiority of some historic instruments, and the myths and legends they have accrued. The literature shows a plethora of wasted scientific effort directed at unanswerable questions by scientists who should have known better. Little can be achieved without solid, reliable measurement, and such data cannot be elicited from human feelings; there can never be a metric description for human responses and relationships, especially those associated with feel, touch and a host of other subjective attributes. The question as to why a player prefers one instrument over another cannot be answered in any meaningful way. Equally as subtle as the relationship between a musical instrument and its player, is the relationship between the player and the maker. The same nuances of feel and comfort are the subject of exchanges between the two parties, and where the maker is also a skilled player the dialogue is internal and equally nuanced. I am privileged to have been part of such a relationship in my trumpet-making career, but I know that no matter how satisfying it might have been, it is impossible to quantify. The ineffable is like that.

Musical instrument making has a long tradition of manual craftsmanship, as opposed to the more recent developments of machine manufacture. With almost all the instruments of the orchestra, the finest and most prized are still essentially made by hand, one by one. Large-scale manufacturers will offer a range of products, the costliest being those that have had a greater degree of personal attention in their creation. With these high-end instruments, the maker's tools and techniques imprint the materials with unique qualities. Musicians will assess a number of instruments, to all outward appearances identical, before selecting the one among them that suits them best. The musician is guided by the indefinable signals of feel and preference. Again, a metric description of these sensations is not possible; it is not that kind of data.

In general, most of the musical instrument crafts based in woodwork passed through the 18th and 19th century industrial revolutions unchanged in essence, and one can discern clearly today the antecedents of the crafts in the present-day workshops and their processes. The tools and techniques remain largely unchanged. The exception to this general rule is in instruments made of metal. Here profound changes in fabrication techniques were introduced with such processes as bell spinning, sheet metal rolling, drawing of seamless tubing, development of purer alloys, soldering with gas flames and rotary polishing. Most of these processes have little influence upon the acoustic properties of the finished product, and simply make fabrication quicker and the finished quality more consistent. But not all of them.

When assessing a natural trumpet for desirable playing qualities, hand-making is critical. Imperfections in the bores of hand-crafted metal instruments have an advantageous influence upon tone formation. Reporting on a series of systematic tests on original instruments, natural trumpet pioneer Don Smithers *et al* concluded that:

> In spite of the perfection of modern, machine-made components as opposed to the irregularities in eighteenth century handmade construction, the old instruments are much easier to play and are more in tune than modern facsimiles.[2]

There is an acoustic basis for this observation. Although ease of playing is clearly a subjective phenomenon—as it is based upon perceptions and feelings—the differences between old and new instruments, absent the player, can be measured and recorded. Measurements of these phenomena, and deductions based upon them, are within the realm of scientific enquiry because they involve the assessment of physical parameters within the instruments, in the absence of the idiosyncrasies and nuances of the player's relationship to them. From the findings reported by Smithers *et al*, it is evident that at least one factor in the ability to play in tune is related to the manner and technique of construction; a smooth bore produced from modern machine-made seamless tubing will cause the nodal vibrational points of the air column to be more focused and less amenable to manipulation by the embouchure alone. The measure of acoustic damping within the bore is known as the quality factor (Q). It is lower in less smoothly finished components, but not so low in metal instrument tubing as to cause the harmonics to sound fuzzy and unfocused. This imperfection, introduced by human intervention during the manufacturing process, results in an instrument more accommodating to the idiosyncratic requirements of playing in tune.[3]

Another related, and perhaps equally significant, feature of a trumpet's acoustic makeup is the method of assembly. Each section of the historic natural trumpet is inserted into the following section by means of a tapered joint; one end is opened out and the other is squeezed in to accommodate it.[4] In modern instrument construction the tubes are butted end-to-end with no step. Tapering the joints was done to facilitate repair, as dismantling such joints is far easier than undoing solder. As a result, there are four steps in the bore between the components, and further steps are introduced at the mouthpiece and by any tuning bits or crooks that may be inserted. These features—not seen in instruments assembled using modern methods—also have the effect of lowering Q, the quality factor.

As a craftsman, I support a 'philosophy of imperfection.' It has a parallel in the 19th century movements that championed craftsmanship and rejected the dehumanizing processes of machine manufacture. Such social commentators as John Ruskin and William Morris urged a return to manually-based actions, which produced objects that possessed vitality because of their very imperfection. Ruskin propounds the dignity of manual work and argues for handcrafted products that show tacit evidence of healthy and ennobling labour.[5] Although perhaps it's my flight of fancy, there is certainly a sense of harmony in a relationship between spirit and handcraft that predates the industrial ethos of the brass instruments of the modern commercial baroque orchestra.

These observations on tone formation and flexibility provide very solid evidence for the superiority of the original construction methods and techniques, which leads to a sound argument for making copies in the original way.

There's a beguiling philosophical parallel where the music of the 17th and 18th centuries is performed in harmonious balance with instruments that have been built according to the technology and craft practices of the period. In the case of the trumpet, this would signify a return to what is considered normal instrument-making practice among the greater proportion of the instruments of the baroque orchestra. The return to a tradition with solid antecedents.

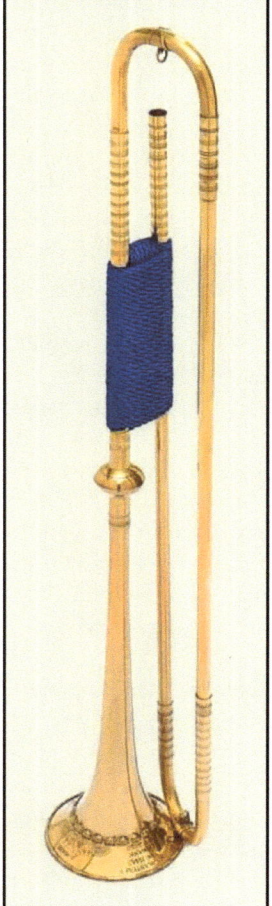

Figure 9 (above): Close-up of the garland of the instrument shown on the left.

Figure 10 (left): Copy by Nikolai Mäntarri based on a trumpet by J.W. Haas, c. 1710-1720. (Photos courtesy of Nikolai Mäntarri.)

It is gratifying to see a new generation of trumpet-makers taking the ideas of honest hand-work and traditional techniques to heart, producing trumpets than can hold their own with the finely crafted instruments found for years in the ranks of the strings and woodwinds.

It's nothing more than simple good taste.

Notes

[1] Barclay, R., *The Preservation and Use of Historic Musical Instruments* (London: Earthscan, 2004), pp. 41-48.

[2] Smithers, D., Wogram, K. and Bowsher, J., 'Playing the Baroque Trumpet,' *Scientific American*, 254:4 (1986), pp. 109-115.

[3] Taping over the holes of a machine-made vented trumpet can simulate the real thing, and some makers supply little screws or corks to close the holes. But it is debatable whether machine-made components will behave as well as a handmade ones. I am no authority.

[4] This is so for Continental instruments. English instruments employ butt joints, often sealed with waxed thread in a similar way to woodwinds.

[5] Ruskin, J., *The Stones of Venice* (Vol. I) (Orpington, Kent: George Allen, 1886).

Chapter Six
Teaching Others

> How do I make an instrument? Well, I just hit the metal with a hammer until it looks like a trumpet, and then stop. Silly bloody question.
>
> R. Barclay (attrib)

What better way to introduce the natural trumpet to musicians, teachers, students and enthusiasts than having them make one for themselves? Although this sounds like a great idea in principle, it is actually fraught with difficulties. When the idea was first proposed to me by Rick Seraphinoff in 1993, I considered it impossible; risible in fact. I had calculated then that I spent approximately 23 hours making an instrument, and therefore could not visualize leading unskilled people, no matter how enthusiastic, in doing the same in anything less than twice that time. And what about the logistics of the thing? No, not an option. I didn't allow for two factors: Rick's persuasive powers and my latent desire for challenge. So, why not try it? Why not bring together eight participants, tell them right up front that the chances of them finishing anything that even looked like—let along played like—a natural trumpet was remote, and have them go at it? You can imagine me, then, sitting back with arms crossed in the music school auditorium in Bloomington, Indiana, on a Saturday afternoon at the end of a long and arduous week, and hearing Biber's *Sonata Sancti Polycarpi* played on eight natural trumpets with organ continuo! It's been played better, I will admit, but good Lord, had we *ever* underestimated the capacity of enthusiasts, together with our own capabilities in showing them what to do!

Mind you, if the detractors of the International Trumpet-making Workshop could examine those first efforts, they might have grist for their mills, but only in terms of the finish. Not wishing to denigrate the work of those first participant/guineapigs, their handiwork was... less than attractive. But the point is that if one has the dimensions of the mandrels correct, the parts formed on them will be of a very high precision, no matter who is performing the work. One is working here in thousandths of an inch so, even with a lack of craft skill, the result *must* conform to fine tolerances. Thus, it is possible to predict that the resultant instrument will have commensurate properties to the original, and this was the case.

I considered that 1994 workshop to be the first and the last. Surely, I thought, we have scoured North America for crazies, and there could hardly be any more. At the opening of the 1995 Bloomington workshop, I made the following statement: 'After last year's workshop I swore I would never do another one. This is it.' It still took the full working week and half the following Saturday to complete another batch of instruments, and their quality matched those of the year before. But they played.

It astonishes me now that we considered offering these workshops with the tooling I had at the time. There was one bell mandrel—derived from the Hanns Hainlein instrument I mentioned earlier—one set of the specialized jigs and forms, and precious few other tools of any kind. All of it went into a wooden box in the back of my car that I drove for 16 hours from Ottawa to Bloomington. We borrowed workspace in the university's silversmithing shop and made a hell of a noise throughout the building with our hammering. We had no drawbench for forming the tubes, so we forced them (slightly undersized) onto their mandrels with brute force. Oh, it was a seat-of-the-pants affair.

Trumpet player and teacher Friedemann Immer heard about our workshop and invited us to stage one in 1996 at the Sweelinck Konservatorium in Amsterdam. While it had been madness to even consider a North American workshop, it was doubly so to take it overseas to an unknown venue in the days when the fastest form of communication was the fax. So, we agreed. The back and forth in organizing this one week of work was prodigious, culminating in a memorable message from the Netherlands following a long silence from them: 'Don't worry. If you hear nothing from us, it means everything is okay.' Shipping the tools ahead was not an option as I was using them regularly for my own trumpet-making, so the wooden box and I had to fly on the same KLM plane to Amsterdam. The relief I felt when I went to claim the box at customs was immense. Then there was the issue of taxis; the damned thing was so heavy that several drivers baulked at the idea of driving me anywhere. I think the epitome of disorganization came when we discovered that we didn't have enough sheet metal. This was due to a slight miscalculation of the number of participants. By the mercy of the trumpet-making gods, Rick's bell supplier from Markneukirchen happened to be planning a visit to Amsterdam, and was persuaded to include some brass in his luggage. His knowing smile spoke volumes about our little game.

Somehow, Rick and I pulled the whole workshop together and ended a week with another group of happy customers—12 this time—and another batch of instruments that will have organologists two centuries from now asking some serious questions.

Friedemann Immer followed the success of this workshop by hosting another the year after, this time back-to-back with one sponsored and organized by Edward Tarr. The fact that these workshops were hosted by the two chief protagonists of the 'other school' speaks volumes for the breadth of their commitment.[1] We will be forever honoured by their interest and enthusiasm. Edward Tarr's workshop was hosted by Frank Bär at the Germanisches Nationalmuseum in Nürnberg. This was in the very laboratory where I had studied in 1977 and, of course, in the city that produced the lion's share of the brass instruments of the Renaissance and Baroque. That year we established the 'new tradition' of making and donating an instrument to the hosting organization as a way of saying thank you. So, it was with enormous pleasure that I engraved MACHT ROB︁T BARCLAI I︁N NÜRNBERG MCMXCVII around the garland, together with three stylized steaming bratwursts in commemoration of a dinner the organizers had hosted.

It was in this second Amsterdam workshop that Rick and I met Michael Münkwitz, one of the participants, who finished his trumpet gorgeously at around midday on Wednesday. It was only a few years later that I met Michael again in the company of Friedemann Immer, who proposed that Michael organize a workshop in Rostock, Germany, his home town. Michael audited a workshop the next year in Edinburgh, hosted by Arnold Myers of the Edinburgh University Collection of Historic Musical Instruments, and acted as teaching assistant. He was obviously going to be 'our man in Europe,' and so the present-day International Trumpet-making Workshop (ITW) was born with Rostock as its European base.

Figure 11: A week's production from the Edinburgh workshop of 2002.

Once the European and North American workshops were established, it was three sessions a year—sometimes four—with around 12 participants in each. Aside from Rostock and Bloomington, our two *pieds-a-terre*, we have visited Amsterdam (Netherlands); Edinburgh, Stapleford and Linton (UK); Nürnberg and Schwerin (Germany); Mynämäki (Finland); Brussels

(Belgium); and Kremsmünster, Schärding and Graz (Austria). At the time of writing there have been 72 workshops with a total of 816 trumpets being turned out. The popularity of our workshop, which we still find astounding, is testified by the number of participants who return, sometimes more than once. These we call our repeat-offenders.

As the workshop developed, so did the tooling. Refined hand tools, and lots more of them, were joined by individual toolboxes, a drawbench, dedicated lathes, jigs, engravers, stamps and other devices, along with streamlined procedures. The workshop is now completed by mid-Friday, and the decorative aspect and finish of the instruments is a vast improvement on those first few. The social media presence of the workshops was also enhanced with website entries featuring detailed information and videos.[2]

A key point to be emphasised is that all the information we possess is free for the asking; there are no closely-guarded secrets, no techniques we withhold. Participants are free to take dimensions from our mandrels and patterns, and our textbook (see next page) illustrates every aspect of the process. The drawing alone is the property of the museum that holds the instrument.

Two features of the later workshops are noteworthy. The first feature is the music. While on the ferry in 2007 from Rostock to Hanko in Finland, Rick sat down with ruled paper and pencil and wrote the *Hainlein Suite*, a *Musikalische Darstellung des Trompetenbaus*. It is in six movements, each named for an activity during the week, and each reflecting the actions of the day (such as *Anvil Chorus*), with a final triumphant fanfare. Like most period trumpet ensemble music, the suite is in four parts so there's a role from the most accomplished high players right down to pedestrians like me. The *Hainlein Suite* is now a fixture on our closing day.[3]

Figure 12: The first movement, Fanfare, of the Hainlein Suite.

The second feature is our workshop manual. Initially, we had produced a manual using photographs taken during our second Edinburgh workshop and printed by our hosts there, for which we were very grateful.[4] The preponderance of workshops in German-speaking locations convinced us that a bilingual text was in order. The present textbook is the result.[5] Many hundreds of copies have been sold, aside from the ones that are provided free to all participants.

There are a few musical highlights that will always stay in my mind. At the close of the Nürnberg workshop, Ed Tarr organized a public concert in the Germanisches Nationalmuseum musical instrument galleries, performed on the workshop trumpets accompanied by a positive organ from the collection. There were some fine players in the group that year, and I think this was the first time we really understood that we were teaching people to make proper musical instruments.

Quite a few years later we had a playing session in Schärding, Austria, which was also memorable. On that occasion there was a core of professional players, led by Jean-François Madeuf, and we had a pair of original baroque tympani. The *Hainlein Suite* had never been played better, and it was then that Rick realized that his composition most certainly had musical merit. As for me, I had played the natural trumpet with the best in the world... Recently, I got out my hammer and torch and made a pair of tympani based on those originals, to accompany the trumpets, so now we can give our participants in Bloomington a really rousing send-off.

Figure 13: Our pair of baroque tympani based upon 18th century originals.

I think the finest moment in my ITW experience was at our workshop in 2006 at Schloss Kremsegg in Kremsmünster, Austria. At the close of the workshop our host, Franz Streitwieser, organized a banquet in the quadrangle, and he had located in the archives some trumpet music that had been written for the schloss in 1660. It was a mild evening with a clear sky, the first few stars were making their presence known, and there was good food and lots of Austrian red wine flowing. All of this created an ambience that made the musical finale—played in the very place it was written, on the kind of instrument for which it was intended—a profoundly moving experience.

Ah, how we old trumpet-makers do go on... Drink's a terrible thing.

Notes

[1] Ed and Friedemann had both pioneered the use of vented instruments over very long careers.

[2] http://trompetenmacher.de/de/allgemein/workshop/; https://www.seraphinoff.com/about-the-international-trumpet-making-workshops

[3] I show just one movement of the suite here as an example. After editing, this music and other pieces written specifically for the ITW trumpets will appear on imslp.org.

[4] Seraphinoff, R., Parks, R., Nex, J. and Barclay, R., *Making a Natural Trumpet* (Edinburgh: Edinburgh University Collection of Historic Musical Instruments, 2003)

[5] Münkwitz, M., Seraphinoff, R. and Barclay, R., *Making a Natural Trumpet/ Herstellung einer Naturtrompete* (Ottawa: Loose Cannon Press, 2014) (See Postamble, p. 60.)

Chapter Seven
Copying and Reproduction

> Copying offers an important means of grasping how an original instrument was designed, built, and intended to work, and a copy can serve as a springboard for further development.
>
> Laurence Libin, *The Grove Dictionary of Musical Instruments*

In a long career as a museum conservator and trumpet-maker, I have accumulated what I like to think of as wisdom, but what is more likely to be mere information. But to continue from discussions of craftsmanship and teaching other people the basics of what I have learned, I'd like to get into some of the processes of turning the information possessed by a museum piece into a working trumpet.[1]

You get a lot more out of a copy of a historic musical instrument than you do from a restored original. This is because the effects of deterioration on materials, and the alterations made during servicing and changes of musical fashion, can be 'reversed' by using new materials, and thus recreating the state of the instrument when new. This is not to say that restoration of original instruments has no place in modern practice, but the musical results of restoration cannot be relied upon. This is because the extent and manner of restoration depends on the state of knowledge at the time. A restoration considered 'state of the art' decades ago can seem quite ill-informed if new knowledge and understanding has come to light.[2] The *'urtext'* of the object—what a restorer considers the instrument looked like when new—is always a 'moving target,' and so successive phases of restoration actually drive the historic instrument further from its primary state, not nearer. Naturally, copying the existing state of an instrument has the same problems, but at least the original remains intact.

This being said, of all the historic instruments that have come down to us, trumpets in their simplicity are often less buggered-about that most. One exception provides a salutary lesson: I was testing instruments in a museum with a French colleague when we came across a restoration horror show. It looked as if an amateur plumber had been at it with a coarse file, a handful of nondescript brass fittings, a blowtorch, and about a pint of lead solder. Such treatment should have been a flogging offence. The tragedy was that the instrument was amazingly in tune. *'C'est juste!'* my colleague cried. *'C'est incroyable, mais c'est juste!'*

But this trumpet was impossible to copy.

Playing and Preservation

The debate over restoring to playability versus static conservation has raged for years, with the entrenchment of warring camps. There is much gossip among musicians and instrument makers upon the so-called intransigence and conservatism of museum personnel. It should not exist in the present day, but it was come by honestly years ago. The so-called white-gloved, anal-retentive spoilsports are reactionary figures spawned from long ago when gung-ho 'restorers'—who were often not qualified to run a pub-garden whelk stand—went roaring through musical instrument collections leaving a trail of sawdust and shattered technical history. I have seen enough historic instruments ruined by restoration to side with their attitude, but by now it should all be in the past. Decades-long developments in the philosophy and technology of museum object conservation have shown there's a middle road, where you can restore to playability while still maintaining conservation standards.[3]

Figures 14 & 15: My good friends the restorer and the conservator, both characters spawned from an ancient polarity, and now gone with the dodo.

In my experience, these negative attitudes towards hands-off curatorial and conservation staff are now outdated. I haven't encountered any of this antagonism recently, and have always been pleasantly surprised at the welcome I and my colleagues have received wherever we have gone. It's clear to me that the custodians consider access to their collections of prime importance. It must be remembered that they do not *own* these historic objects; they are their custodians, and it is in the best interest of both their institutions and the public to make access as convenient as possible, within the strictures of good curatorship and conservation. Even though the objects themselves are in their care, and the collections hold copyright, the information those objects possess is in the public domain.

Like all historic objects, instruments need protection while being studied and measured, and international protocols for this purpose have been formulated.[4] There are several particular risks to metal instruments: handling of sensitive surfaces can result in tarnishing or deeper corrosion, careless handing can result in dents and scratches, and there can be stimulation of corrosion in interiors exposed to warm, moist breath. Measuring tools and techniques should be non-invasive, safe handling procedures should be followed, and sounding or playing sessions should be conducted with certain specified restrictions. None of this is onerous, and to follow an individual museum's guidelines is simply respectful of the personnel and of the object under study.

There's a distinction between 'soundability' and 'playability.' 'Soundable' means that the instrument can be played for the sake of assessing pitch, timbre and other features, whereas playability means just that. Naturally, the distinction between these two is subjective, but with trumpets, the distinction centres on the condition of the metal. Surprisingly, small dents in tubing have very little effect on the playing quality of an instrument. However, brass that has been highly stressed during forming has a tendency to become brittle and crack because corrosion—usually from exposure to alkalis—attacks and weakens the metal's grain boundaries. The resultant deterioration is known as season cracking, and it is irreversible. Brass in this condition must be handled very carefully as the cracks have a tendency to get worse under further stress. Playing instruments in this condition is not wise.

Figure 16: Typical stress corrosion on a horn bell. (Photo courtesy of R. Seraphinoff.)

Once a playing session is finished, it has been routine practice to dry the interior of the instrument with airflow to prevent any dormant interior corrosion from being initiated.[5] Highly polished exteriors look very fine, but the interior condition of instrument's bores is often a deep mystery. Leave well enough alone is a wise course. Recently, a team of researchers at the Berner Fachhochschule in Bern, Switzerland have found that drying by airflow is quick and efficient, while moisture left in instruments after playing will remain for a considerable length of time.[6] When I visited, they were working on a small device that consisted of a fan connected to a mouthpiece taper, which could be inserted in the instrument's receiver.

The Informed Copy

There are close copies and there are copies made for current musical performance. In the case of historic natural trumpets, what constitutes a copy in the commercial world has been left to a great deal of interpretation, as we know. For the purposes of this section, a copy is defined as an instrument that closely follows the original pattern, and plays and sounds as much like the original as possible. Thus, whatever idiosyncrasies the original has will—we hope—be reflected in the copy. Modification or improvement makes the so-called copy an adaptation, and thus it's useless in understanding the original. I think the term 'informed copy' is better than such terms as 'exact' or 'accurate;' a one-to-one replica of a historic object can be approached but never achieved, whereas 'informed' can be defined and standardized, as it has been in the music performance world. The object of the informed copy is an attempt to understand past practices on their own terms.[7]

The accuracy of transferring dimensions between a historic instrument and its copy relies upon the techniques and the skill of the measurer. Calipers, rulers and micrometers are used, although there appears to be no general consensus on degree of accuracy. In recent years, bore measuring devices with solid-state components have become more economical and have increased in accuracy. In general, length measurements of the larger components to an accuracy of 1.00mm are sufficient, but the wall thickness of historic instruments needs an accuracy an order of magnitude greater. With all early brass instruments there are additional complications in the original choice of material. Modern brass is available in finely controlled thicknesses, but the craftsman of centuries ago would rely on the skill of his supplier and his own judgement. Before the era of rolling mills, sheet brass was hammered to an approximate thickness then scraped to achieve consistency.[8] So, measurements taken today of wall thickness are only as good as the skills of the brass scraper who prepared the sheet and the discernment of the instrument-maker who chose it. The sheet brass used in 17th and 18th century instruments will have a degree of variability. An error in measuring original thicknesses within 0.10mm would be acceptable in these circumstances. Here is one area where the modern copyist makes a compromise; averaging a number of measurements results in the choice of one modern, consistent thickness.

There's a further complication in the replication of mandrels. The steel mandrel on which tubes and bells are formed must conform exactly to their inside diameters, so wall thickness of the metal must be added. This is a simple calculation for cylindrical tubing: deducting twice the thickness of the material from the overall diameter of the tube. The bell, on the other hand, is thinner at its extremity due to the process of manufacture. Often, it is impossible to measure the thickness of the metal at the bell's extremity because it is covered by a reinforcing garland. When this thickness can be measured it is possible to estimate the dimensions of the flat pattern used in laying out the bell. This is a trial-and-error process, and I know of no calculation that makes it easier.

While working on an internship at the Germanisches Nationalmuseum in 1977, I made a number of technical drawings of brass instruments in the collection, including one of a set of three trumpets by Johann Leonard Ehe III from 1746. This drawing has been a quite popular request from the museum. A later visit confirmed the excellent playing quality of these instruments, but I was well aware earlier that a drawing can never tell instrument-makers all they need to know. Producing drawings has been an excellent way of sharing information and providing remote access to collections, but transferring measurements from the original to the drawing, then taking the measurements from the drawing remotely, inevitably results in transcription errors. For the musical instrument-maker who is supplying a market, this is not a significant issue, as it is often necessary to make minor (and sometimes major) adjustments for best results. This 'tweaking' is a common occurrence,

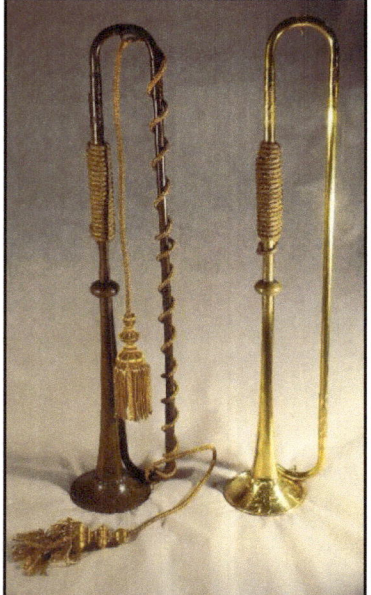

and it is here that accomplished instrumentmakers establish and maintain their creativity. On the other hand, a copy used for comparison purposes requires a direct relationship between the instrument and the copyist. You need them side-by-side. This was the case with a copy I made some years ago of a trumpet by Johann Carl Kodisch dated 1719.[9]

Figure 17: The Kodisch instrument and its copy side by side.

Making one single instrument is an expensive and complex process, because it requires one-off, individual mandrels and forms. In fact, a mandrel that I had used in the 1980s for copies of the undated Kodisch trumpet in the Germanisches Nationalmuseum (MI 163) proved to be subtly different from the one required for this instrument. The tubes of the 1719 trumpet were also found to be slightly narrower. It was interesting to encounter these variations because they tend to suggest a much less conservative approach to workshop tooling than I had previously assumed. Bell mandrels were difficult and time-consuming items to make, so a change in design that necessitated a new form was quite a surprise.[10]

 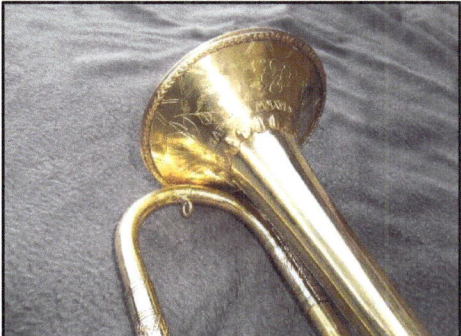

Figure 18 (left): Detail of the garland during engraving. Figure 19 (right): the bell.

On this copy, as many workshop processes as possible followed original practice. The embossed pattern on the ferrules of the Kodisch trumpet would have been produced originally by a supplier using a rolling mill. In the absence of this equipment, dies were laser-cut to reproduce the pattern, and the sheet metal was pressed into them to form an exact facsimile. The bell garland decoration was stamped and engraved in the original manner, with the addition of my name as a little amusement for posterity.[11]

Hammering

We cannot leave the subject of historical techniques without a reference to hammering. Belting away at the metal on an anvil is the one quintessential action of the trumpet-maker. It is illustrated in multiple places in the literature, even though hammering occupies only about 5% of the time taken in making an instrument, and only the top 10cms of the bell is dealt with in this way. Because of this graphic representation—or perhaps in spite of it—there has been a great deal of fatuous speculation on the technique's ability to impart a magical and hitherto unsuspected quality to the acoustics of the finished instrument. This is bullshit, and here's why.

Think about it (or you can read what I've already written[12]): when brass is hammered, or any other stressing and straining treatment is applied to it, it becomes 'work hardened.' The granular property of the metal is distorted. Once this state is achieved, the metal must be heated close to red-heat in order to soften it. If we continue working the hardened brass it can split. Then, when heated, the distortion in the grains that resulted in hardening is eliminated, and the metal returns to a soft, poly-crystalline state in which none of the previous treatment can be detected. One can still *see* the hammer marks, of course, but that is purely visual. The metal has been changed. Thus, one can hammer the metal, burnish it, draw it and bend it, or even whack it with a rolled-up newspaper, it makes no difference.

When the bell's end had been hammered to approximately the right size on the anvil, the bell is then softened, placed on the mandrel and burnished heavily to bring it into intimate contact. Again, phases of reheating and cooling take place. I prefer to finish the bell with a round of burnishing, and not reheat it, thus leaving it in a hard state. That hard state has absolutely nothing to do with the hammering that took place much earlier.

Therefore, if you see a newly-made natural trumpet that displays hammer marks you can draw one of two conclusions: 1) the instrument has been very poorly finished through haste or lack of skill; or 2) the hammer marks have been left, or even applied after completion, to convince you of their magic properties. Cry 'Aroint thee, witch. Aroint thee, and take yourself hence!' We have no business here believing in magic.

Choice of Materials

This is a huge topic and I have no intention of going into it in great detail. I have two good reasons: firstly, from my slender knowledge of the subject, I couldn't do it justice; and, secondly, the literature abounds with scholarly treatment of the topic. So, what follows are a few observations gleaned from my experience.

Newly created 'Nürnberg brasses' have been used by instrument-makers in which lead—which is found as a trace impurity in the original material—has been reintroduced into the modern copper/zinc alloy. It's hoped this will produce detectable musical results. There has been a great deal of analysis of historic brasses and speculation on their acoustic properties in the last few decades, but conclusions on the resultant playing qualities that withstand scientific rigour are hard to find. In a recent study, the authors conclude:

> In spite of intensive research and considerable progress in this field, one of the most persistent questions still remains: What is the significance for historically informed performance of the use of a historically correct alloy in reproductions of brasswind musical instruments?[13]

In my opinion, this question will never be answered satisfactorily because the acoustic measurements are, firstly, an order of magnitude less significant than the idiosyncrasies of individual players and their embouchures; and, secondly, and much more important, those very idiosyncrasies—their likes and dislikes, feelings and beliefs—are not, and never will be, subject to scientific analysis. They will always be 'Diagrammatic caricatures of the ineffable.'[14] However, if some serious and systematic double-blind tests were to be organized under rigorous scientific protocols, we might get nearer to an answer. A series of such tests was organized almost a century ago to challenge the vaunted superiority of the Cremona violins.[15] The results: nobody, player or audience member, could tell the difference between old fiddles and new ones. Nevertheless, nearly 100 years later, the mythology of superiority persists and flourishes in spite of this, and later, concrete evidence to the contrary. (There is, of course, a vested interest in a status quo that assigns values in the millions.) So, I hold no illusions that a similar series of tests on various brasses will fare any better. That's because we're dealing with human beings and all their foibles. On the other hand, if a systematic series of tests did show that brasses made to original recipes were more suited to early instrument-making than modern materials, I would be delighted.

However, regardless of whether some scientific investigation can produce reliable numbers, these very idiosyncrasies play an extremely important part in a musician's choice of instrument. Players have stated that instruments made recently using so-called *Nürnberger Blech* play differently. These are subjective evaluations, of course, but I can't downplay or ignore their significance to the player. As I said in Chapter Five, the relationship between a musical instrument and its player is one of the subtlest of all human interactions. If the player believes there is a difference, then there is. Assigning numbers will neither elucidate nor clarify. And the same for thoughtless scepticism.

With all this in mind, a 0.40mm (0.016") brass sheet of 70% copper and 30% zinc is generally used for most copies. Some European makers favour an alloy of 72% copper and 28% zinc. Around 30% of zinc is at the high end of what was possible by the early process of cementation, where zinc vapour was allowed to diffuse into molten copper. Few original brass founders achieved this high level, but Nürnberg makers certainly selected material sourced from mines that were known for the purity of their ores, and treated by foundries and hammer mills that had high control over the quality of their sheet metal. The brasses used by the Nürnberg craftsmen are of remarkable purity but have variable consistency, showing a wide range of zinc content over the centuries of their production. This range of zinc uptake in the founding process poses the knotty question of *which* alloy one should use for *which* historical copy.[16]

If all other features of the copied instrument are approached with high attention to authentic practice, use of 'Nürnberg brass'—however it is defined and quantified—will put the proverbial icing on the cake.

Notes

[1] More detailed sections of this chapter appear in *Hinter den Tönen: Muikinstrumente als Forschungsgebeit*, pp. 142-147. (Nürnberg: Germanisches Nationalmuseum, 2018.)

[2] Barclay, R., 'Ethics in the Conservation and Preservation of Brass Instruments,' *Historic Brass Society Journal*, Vol. 1, 1989, pp. 75-81.

[3] Watson, J., *Artifacts in Use* (Richmond, VA: OHS Press/Colonial Williamsburg, 2010).

[4] CIMCIM, 1985.

[5] Barclay, Robert (ed), *The Care of Historic Musical Instruments* (Edinburgh: CCI/CIMCIM/MGC, 1997) p. 103.

[6] Von Steiger, A., et al., 'New Insights into the Conservation of Brass Instruments,' *Historic Brass Society Journal*, Vol. 30, 2018, pp. 85-101.

[7] An excellent example of an instrument-maker's thinking in producing informed copies is available at: http://www.seraphinoff.com/content.php?p=6c3bfe89-1bf6-40f9-9d95-db4bcb87f03f

[8] Barclay *op cit* (1992) pp. 50-51.

[9] Clements, S. and Barclay, R., 'Discovery of a Previously Unrecorded Trumpet by Johann Carl Kodisch,' *Historic Brass Society Journal*, Vol. 29, 2017, pp. 69-79.

[10] I'm sure one of my detractors will say it shouldn't have been.

[11] I am indebted to Scott Clements for permission to publish this section and the accompanying photographs.

[12] 'Some Bubbles Prick'd: A Discussion of Early Brass Mythology,' *Perspectives in Brass Scholarship: Proceedings of the International Historic Brass Symposium*, Amherst, 1995, ed. S. Carter (Stuyvesant, NY: Pendragon, 1997), pp. 73-74.

[13] Vereecke, H., W., Frühmann, B. and Schreiner, M., 'The Chemical Composition of Brass in Nuremberg Trombones of the Sixteenth Century,' *Historic Brass Society Journal*, Vol. 24, 2012, p. 71.

[14] Wells, H. G., Dr Gipfel in *The Chronic Argonauts*.

[15] Chenantais, J., *Le violoniste et le violon* (Nantes: L. Durance Libraire Ancienne et Modern, 1927)

[16] Data on this issue are very well summarized in Vereecke H., *The Sixteenth-century Trombone: Dimensions, Materials and Techniques*, (Turnhout: Brepols, 2016) pp. 165-175.

Chapter Eight
Getting Inside the Tradition

> The test of first-rate intelligence is the ability to hold
> two opposed ideas in the mind at the same time, and
> still retain the ability to function.
> F. Scott Fitzgerald, 'The Crack Up' (*Esquire*)

Back to the invented tradition of the vented trumpet. The history and development of this instrument has given me fascinating insights into how a canon of practice develops. How did an instrument that is musically, acoustically and taxonomically inappropriate in its context gain ascendency and become the standard of the new baroque orchestra? So far, I have described what happened when the tradition was being invented, but if we dig deeper into the social forces driving the change, we see a clearer picture. It's a really nice picture, too; one of hardworking people being inventive and creative while under pressure to keep work coming their way. Not drivers, but driven. It is not constructive to criticize the current state of affairs without understanding the incremental societal developments that drove the change. I used to be highly critical of the early phases of the process, but I have no regrets on that score because the products and their use were so grossly inappropriate to my ideas of refinement, balance and sensitivity in baroque music. They were rubbish. However, there's been a lot of water under the bridge since then.

Placing the actions of the practitioners in their historical and social context provides a more balanced and rational view, especially if we include two important aspects among the societal drivers: a cadre of insatiable egos who stand up at the front, wag a stick and have it all their own way; and an industry—in effect, a baroque music factory—that requires the absolute perfection that only machines can provide. And wouldn't it be a wonderful world if more players could specialize in the natural trumpet and make a living doing it? The reality is vastly different, and baroque gigs are just one aspect of busy musical lives.

There are two facets of the vented trumpet that we can look at from a social perspective, inside the tradition as it were: the static visual aspect of the instrument and its practical musical operation.

How it Looks

An intriguing aspect of the vented trumpet's development and presentation is not primarily a musical one; it is visual. I cannot emphasize enough how important appearances are. If the prime consideration were auditory, the tone colour of the coiled instruments that Helmut Finke and Otto Steinkopf invented in 1961 would have been considered intolerable, but it was not. (We find it intolerable today.) There is a strong argument to be made for a sensitivity to the outward appearance of the instrumentation; the player's trumpet must 'look right' to the audience. If this were not the case, valved instruments with 18th century pitch and bore specifications could well have been developed further; being without vents, their air columns would more closely replicate the original acoustical function and tone colour of the natural instrument.[1] But visual impressions are among the most powerful of the senses, and outweigh the auditory in their level of discrimination among the general populace. We go to *see* a concert. Thus, watching players operating valves—no matter how subtly—would clash with the visual desire for the exotic and different.

The coiled instrument developed in the 1960s had its supporting counterpart in the Haussmann portrait, and thus its appearance on the concert stage or in pictures on record sleeves might well be viewed as authentic through its appeal as 'other.' In a similar way, when the long, one-looped trumpet with ventholes was developed, the holes could be subtly manipulated without great visual compromise, especially when located on the back bow. Indeed, well into the 21st century, educators were still counselling students on subtlety in opening and closing the vents, clearly indicating the importance of falsifying appearances, and also, incidentally, presenting their students with a moral dilemma.[2] What other course in academia actively encourages cheating?

You could also see examples of fudging in players' portraits on record notes where they were sometimes posed with a hand curled around the area of the trumpet where the tone holes lay. In the most egregious examples, separate takes of videos were made where the trumpeters adopted the classical one-handed stance and mimed to the music. This was downright naughty. Interestingly, it was soon discovered in Continental trumpet-making practice that it was much more convenient to locate the vents on a crook inserted into the back bow, thus creating a double-looped instrument with replaceable vent sections of varying lengths. Such was the legitimization of the vented instrument by this time, that the visual aspect could be sacrificed for convenience.

At the close of the International Trumpet-making Workshop, the playing session on the completed instruments is always a satisfying and emotionally moving experience, as the instructors absorb the delight of the participants with the products of their own hands. But it's always amusing to watch how some of them adopt the classic one-handed stance when playing, while others poise a hand upon the tubing of the lower yard. You can even detect little movements of the fingers sometimes, evocative to me of the slight, vestigial twitches of what ought to become a dying ethos.

Making it Work

Practical musical operation both defined and refined the vented trumpet. In the classical music performance canon, renewal and reinterpretation are normal values. Among many examples is the groundbreaking work, alluded to earlier, of Glenn Gould in the interpretation of much of J. S. Bach's oeuvre for harpsichord. There is no useful argument to be made on grounds of inauthenticity, even though the music is played upon an instrument that was in its infancy during Bach's period, and was specifically not used by him. When pianist Alicia de Rocha (1923-2009) was asked if she had performed Beethoven's works on a contemporary instrument—a Broadwood, for example—she stated that it was impossible. Her opinion was that Beethoven foresaw the modern grand piano in his writing, and this was '…the reason why he composed his best music after he had gone deaf.'[3] Although this is a complete howler, it underscores the view that the original instrument doesn't matter a hoot. The grand piano is the bridging tool between the composer and the player, and its nature and function are valued for their musical result in the modern context.

The same argument can be made for the use of the piccolo trumpet in playing baroque works; it is the tool that modern players may use safely and reliably for presenting their interpretations of the work. There is no desire in the classical music canon of performance to hark back to earlier technologies. Simply put, the choice of the tool is made through practical musicianship in the modern world.

The Early Music Movement changed all this; it was a radical break with tradition in an era when comfortable norms were falling by the wayside. It cracked the classical canon, and two clear sides emerged; those breaking with the old, and those holding fast to it. Among many battles over the years, there was one particularly silly exchange of words between Pinchas Zukerman of the National Arts Centre Orchestra in Ottawa and Jeanne Lamon of Toronto's Tafelmusik. Mr Zukerman had stated that all historic performance was 'rubbish,' which convinced Ms Lamon that he had, indeed, had his head buried in the sand for the last 30 years. Ms Lamon proposed a musical duel, but the challenge was never taken up.[4] I thought it highly ironic to run the early music company banner up the flagpole, knowing the sort of plumbing fittings that were considered acceptable in Tafelmusik's band. Talk about the pot calling the kettle black!

There was much sensible resistance to the development of compromised trumpets since experiments began,[5] but practical musicianship carried much more force. The idea of first doing a thing badly, so as to learn to do it well, was very short-lived, especially as 'doing it badly' often involved public exposure. This early period was a time of performances on strange and exotic instruments. They were attractive because of their novelty, while their musical short-comings were forgiven at the expense of the spectacle. I possess a number of unspeakable 33rpm records of Medieval and Renaissance music created from new cloth by a species of academic legerdemain. (There's a book still to be written about that crazy, creative, inventive period!) The nadir of LPs, I think, is the Guillaume de Machaut *Mess de Nostre Dame* backed by krummhorns![6] Our friend the sackbut acquired the name it is now saddled with in the opening years of the Early Music Movement, not because it represented an early type of trombone—there is no historical sackbut extant—but through its beguiling name. Its name is a marker of the attractiveness of 'other' in an age of rejection of canons. It reminded me, years ago, of the music that was played while Shadrach, Meshach and Abednego were deep in the burning fiery furnace.

The term 'fortepiano' is another invented term, coined comparatively recently to distinguish it from the other modern thing, although in what era the historical switch in terms is supposed to take place is anybody's guess. And when does a sackbut become a trombone, as they are essentially the same thing?[7] We don't call it early music now, of course; the current flavour is 'historical performance,' as if there were some year in the past when events suddenly become historical. When is this switch? Stravinsky, Copland, Little Richard, or is it a moving target? We used to wield the term 'authentic' before it became debased beyond recovery, and that was followed by 'historically informed,' although as far as the brasses went, Clio (sagest of the Sisters Nine) wore a gag over her mouth and was blindfolded. But, as a descriptor, 'historical performance' is probably the best we can do for now.

As the record industry boomed with its mass-market appeal, the exotic krummhorns, shawms, rackets and all the other instruments that marked a clear departure from the norm, were avidly seized upon. Many of these were the creations of the incredibly inventive and talented Otto Steinkopf and his followers. This popularity spawned a huge cottage industry of musical instrument-making, with the corollary of throwing musical instrument museum collections open to the willy-nilly scrutiny and intervention with tools that I have discussed earlier. Whether or not the instruments so produced always possessed solid historical antecedents was of secondary consideration: 'Are your instruments original?' 'Oh, yes, *very* original.'

But this seat-of-the-pants musical culture was doomed; the era of silly old buggers scraping away at rebecs began to give way under commercial pressure. Musicians and critics alike moved very quickly away from such experimental music, although—with perhaps grudging thanks to the recording industry—one can still hear early renditions on vinyl of the natural trumpet being wrestled down and forced to conform in an orchestral milieu that was quite unsympathetic to it. Advances in recording technology resulted in high, and quite artificial, performance standards. Amalgamation of repeated 'takes' and even splicing of individual notes gave the recorded version an artificial level of purity. As has often been remarked: 'We all fall from grace at the studio door.' It was inevitable that such accurate musical results, produced painstakingly in the recording studio, would be expected on stage. At the same time, as early music moved out of the phase of exotic curiosity and into a mainstream role, public performance demanded safe, reliable playing. This was made easier when directors and conductors sidestepped the enormous complications of historical temperaments and settled for equal temperament, albeit at 'baroque pitch' of A=415Hz. Naturally, practical musicianship and its *doppelgänger*, musical instrument making and development, rose to the occasion producing the tools to get the job done.

Finally, arising out of one of the most dynamic and creative phases in the history of musical instrument making and performance, and after many painstaking experiments, the vented trumpet was born and given its societal stamp of approval. My tale of two trumpets has nearly reached its conclusion.

Nevertheless, there are players who cannot come to terms with the constructed history of their instrument, and still seek avenues into the past.

Bring on King Henry VIII!

Notes

[1] For example, the experimental piston-valve Baroque Trumpet produced in 1960 by Latzsch of Bremen, Germany, on the design of Bruce Holcomb. See https://robertoades.ca/the-horns/

[2] Barclay *op cit* (1998), p. 10.

[3] Tilson Thomas, M., transcript of an interview on *Concerto*, BBC Television, 22 August 1993.

[4] Lamon, Jeanne, 'So, Mr. Zukerman, you want a fight? How about a battle of the bands?,' *Globe and Mail, Toronto*, April 3rd 2000.

[5] Rassmussen, M., 'Bach Trumpet Madness; or, a Plain and Easy Introduction to the Attributes, Causes and Cure of a Most Mysterious Musical Malady,' *Brass Quarterly*, 5, 1, 1961, pp. 37–40.

[6] Guillaume de Machaut was composing in the mid-14th century, two or three hundred years before the krummhorn appeared. Besides, whining double-reeds in holy service would be an abomination. 'What's that thing that makes a whining noise and turns up at the end?' 'That, madam, is the audience.'

[7] Rick Seraphinoff points out that there are very few things that haven't changed substantially since the mid 15th century, beer and trombones being the exception. They are basically the same now as they were then. Beer is a little more carefully made, but with the same ingredients, and the trombone works in exactly the same way, with a little more precision in its construction.

Chapter Nine
Henry VIII's Motorcycle

> Through tattered clothes great vices do appear; robes and furred gowns hide all… Get thee glass eyes, and like a scurvy politician seem to see the things thou dost not.
> William Shakespeare, *King Lear*

Finally, we come to our main title. Sorry to keep you waiting, but there's still a little more delay as I give you some background. Henry VIII, King of England from 1509 to 1547, was very fond of Elsyng Palace in Enfield. It was originally a manor house, but in Henry's reign it was extensively remodelled by its owner, Sir Thomas Lovell. Henry and his entourage moved frequently between stately houses, foisting themselves and their voracious appetites upon many a sycophantic and almost bankrupted court toady. The sovereign was a very frequent guest at Elsyng Palace and used the place as a base for hunting. It is hardly surprising, therefore, that when Henry was ready to choose his motorcycle it would have to be a Royal Enfield.

The King's two-wheeled steed becomes the epitome of the number of players of the vented trumpet who still grasp at straws in an attempt to justify their practice by analyzing obscure texts, inventing pretexts, and searching hard for any piece of archival flotsam to grasp in the shipwreck of their misplaced yearnings. The most laughable of these was the contention that of course they had vented instruments in the baroque period, but examples have simply failed to survive.[1] It's rather gauche to quote oneself, but I will anyway, because I gave this particular instance the shrift it deserved when I wrote in a footnote: 'Sadly, the motorcycle on which Henry VIII roared around Hampton Court Palace in the 1540s has also failed to survive.'[2]

I thought this a beguiling title for my book.

Though I cite but one instance of this rearguard action here, they were and are legion. This particular aspiration—that the winnowing effect of time has expunged all extant examples and unequivocal records—took place in 1994, but its supporters continue their work, as I have mentioned above. There is a social phenomenon called the selective tradition, which describes and quantifies the effect over time of the retention of some works, objects or ideas, and the discarding or relegating of others. A simple example would be a comparison between the 19th century Romantic invention of Antonio Stradivari, who ran a large and successful factory, and the relegation of Jacob Stainer, who was just a damned good instrument-maker. (Trying to knock Stradivarius off his pedestal is another one of those topics that inflame passions and do nobody any good.[3] I should be restrained.) However, the mechanism of the selective tradition is naturally far more subtle than this, and it is reckless and unscholarly of me to over-simplify. Suffice it to say that it is highly unlikely that such a key element as an entire instrument-playing regimen could 'fail to survive' among the scores of extant instruments lacking any of these features. It could not have been selected out of existence. Sorry. There's the matter of the paperwork: the absence of any solid historical documentation. If the use of vents were prevalent, it seems to me that there ought to exist at least one contemporary method book on the subject. Over several centuries it has been the practice of players to publish descriptions of their instruments and their methodologies. And they don't do it with vague hints and subtle references; they write it in plain words. Surely, *somebody* must have thought: 'I ſay! Thiſ iſ ſo clever that I ſhall pubiſh it for poſterity.' Or perhaps: '𝔐ein 𝔊ott, mein 𝔑ame wird in die 𝔊eſchichte eingehen!'[4]

But nobody did. This is a great loss to scholarship, because this is how so much has been learned on early practice; the sources are legion and although they may be argued over by scholars and players, they are tangible proof of what was going on.

The lack of any concrete evidence of a tone-hole culture surely points to the fact that the practice didn't exist. Revisionism of the kind practised by the tone-hole historians requires proof, and there isn't any. However, I was approached by a serious musicologist at a brass instrument conference who took me aside and educated me on this subject. Apparently, because of rigid trumpet guild exclusivity, such information was a closely guarded secret. Nothing could possibly be disseminated on their arcane practices without threat of severe punishment. Nudge, nudge; wink, wink. This is such an Emmenthal of an argument that one wonders where to begin. Well, it's true that there were closed and exclusive trumpet *kameradschaften* in some principalities in Europe at certain periods of history, but to extend this practice to the whole sweep of the Continent over a span of centuries is tossing factual tidbits into the batter of history like raisins in a spotted dick. Such a conspiracy of silence would make the cover-up of the Hollywood moon landings a piece of cake.

Another intriguing concept is the idea that a mini-slide could have been inserted into the mouthpiece receiver, thus allowing the player to make slight alterations in pitch while playing; a sort of miniature *tromba da tirarsi*.[5] This idea was followed up by borescope examinations of extant instruments where scratches were found consistent with 'something' being inserted in the leadpipe. However, as a trumpet-maker, I feel obliged to ask how one can distinguish between the longitudinal marks made during construction, where the tubes are slid with some energy on and off mandrels, and those made afterwards by the action of whatever putative mechanism there might have been. Of course, one can't distinguish, but I would hope that whatever that inserted 'something' was, it would not be so poorly finished as to leave scratches during operation.

That would confuse later researchers no end.

And even if one were to find some obscure reference in a historic document to the suggestion of a tone hole,[6] extrapolating this discovery to three holes, and then four, with sets of dismountable lower yards or crooks to suit different orchestral pitches, is stretching things just a teensy bit.

I could cite many more cases of plummeting grasps at tree limbs on the rocky overhangs of history, but I think the case has been made. Quick! Stamp on that kick-starter, Your Majesty, before your crotch-rocket disappears in a puff of oily logic!

Notes

[1] 'The English Four-hole System,' presentation at Historic Brass Society Conference, Edinburgh, 1994.

[2] Barclay (1998), footnote p. 13.

[3] Barclay, R., 'The Superior Stradivarius: A Fiction Supported by Bad Science,' *Skeptic*, Vol 16, No 2, 2011, pp. 45-50.

[4] My God, my name will go down in history!

[5] Csiba, J. and G., 'Die Tromba da Tirarsi und ihre Folgen,' *Michaelsteiner Konferenzberichte, Posaunen und Trompeten*, 1998 (Stiftung Kloster Michaelstein, Blankenburg, 2000) pp. 93-103.

[6] There is such a reference in Mitzler's *Musikalische Bibliothek* of 1741 where Johann Georg Hillen describes the trumpet, which does not have holes or slides (the instrument we know from the period). It has been suggested that because he states that the trumpet does not have holes, there must have been one *with* them. I have no opinion on this.

Chapter Ten
So, Now What?

Yes, my guard stood hard when abstract threats too noble to neglect
Deceived me into thinking I had something to protect
Good and bad, I define these terms quite clear, no doubt, somehow
Ah, but I was so much older then. I'm younger than that now.

Bob Dylan, My Back Pages

We live in a world where advertising is a multi-billion-dollar industry. We are pelted, bombarded, assaulted all day and every day by legitimized liars. 'Redesigned from the ground up,' 'Contains keratic-53,' 'Over 25% more effective,' 'Your intimate skin deserves lubritol…' And to convince us of the efficacy of their products, there's some sober cove in a white coat surrounded by lab equipment (notice how the fluid in the bubbling flasks and beakers is always blue?) all dressed up so their fabrications look like science. It's the advertising industry's equivalent of some Nigerian 'prince' phishing for a bank account. The Archiv record label, with its organological dissertations, worked on exactly the same principle all those years ago: if it's dressed like *Musikwissenschaft*, it must be! We're now in an era of 'micro targeted alternative realities' where public figures can work with 'alternative facts' or 'speak their own truth.' The frightful implications of this trend go far beyond the silly business of truth and falsehood with fingerholes, but there is a common thread. In a culture of bare-faced lying, where an industry of millions of employees is devoted to making people think they need the stuff that they don't even know they don't need, it is hardly surprising that economy with the truth would winkle its way in our little community.

Look no further than the magical hammer marks referred to in Chapter Seven, which do absolutely nothing except make a trumpet bell look like a garage experiment. And we can all recall the great fad—now debunked—for improving the playing qualities of brass instruments by dunking them in liquid nitrogen.[1] All schemes for pulling wool over gullible eyes. And, of course, the rebranding of the vented trumpet as the 'baroque' trumpet is the same species of marketing sleight of hand.

At the root of being obliged to rely on fabrication in the place of truth, is the fundamental and timeless fact that professional musicians must play to a certain high and inflexible standard, and if they fail to do so they will not be able to put bread on the table. I remember well one French player telling me of an upcoming natural trumpet gig with a very prestigious Paris baroque orchestra: '*Nous ferions mieux de bien jouer, sinon il invitera les Anglais!*'[2] The onus for the adaptation of instruments to conform with *faux* standards rests, therefore, on the directors of the musical ensembles and the executives of recording companies; in short, the musicians' employers. The salesmen. But the musicians have, perforce, been brought into this false narrative and have been obliged to defend it, and in those videos cited earlier, they have done it willingly.

How does a player deal with the knowledge that what is being portrayed does not accord with Baroque reality? Aside, that is, from getting irritated when people like me mention how nice the natural trumpet sounds, or dare to suggest that the search for historical proofs of vents might be a self-deluding chimera?[3] Because of the very nature of the two side-by-side baroque orchestras, such tension is inevitable. What we have here is a parallel valuation of unlike quantities, which causes cognitive dissonance. There are three chief strategies for reducing this cognitive dissonance according to the classical model formulated in 1957.[4] These are circumspect exposure to conflicting views, changes in behaviour, and changes in cognition. Let's check them out, bearing in mind that the following are my thoughts only, and doubtless ill-informed and naïve.

Circumspect Exposure to Conflicting Views
Much has happened in global communication since 1957. Living inside a silo was never easier with the creation of Web-based resources catering to any and all sets of beliefs, no matter how irrational. We are all in touch with each other through our global community. Chat groups, Facebook pages and the rest have encouraged clusters of species to drink at the same waterhole. I see evidence of this circumspect exposure when I post a comment on-line that might be critical of the vented approach. One can raise quite a storm if one is not careful. Praise of those who do it properly does not necessarily go down well. You have to choose your words circumspectly, otherwise there is a reflex action from your attempt to breach the walls. Shoot the messenger.

There is one strategy that might work, though: you could tear this book into strips and use it for firelighters (assuming you were silly enough to part with good money for it in the first place).

Changes in Behaviour
When playing with other instruments, such changes would mean invoking that higher level in the orchestral hierarchy. Sometimes it works, sometimes it doesn't, but either way (as a jobbing amateur) it's none of my business. Clearly, the behaviour of the vented trumpet player is dictated by the attitude of the controlling forces. After all, they are the ones who have put them in this untenable position in the first place through their commercially-driven choice of purported simplicity. If they insist that their players use bogus tools—their concept of historical performance being demonstrably highly

negotiable—they should read this book. It won't tell them anything they don't know already, of course, but it wouldn't do any harm. Besides, I get royalties. For those folks who have made presentations and statements that give obeisance to the lie—deliberately muddying the issue—they would be in for a profound change of behaviour.

Can they do it? Do they have what it takes? I ask because I believe we've had enough of the fudging from players who should know better. Enough of the presentations where the 'natural' trumpet is 'explained' while being mendaciously and paradoxically confused with a completely different instrument. We all know the vented trumpet is false, but in all conscience, we owe it to our public that they be equally informed.[5] And as for the conductors who must have their players use these things, all I can really say is that their choices have placed them in the same category as those adherents to the old classical canon, who they were supposed to have supplanted in the first flush of the Early Music Movement. Any change of behaviour needs to come from the young-minded. But chronological age is no barrier; Saul was not a young man that day on the road to Damascus…

Whether individual players are versatile enough is another factor, also well out of my purview. And perhaps they're comfortable with things just as they are, being obliged by necessity to play a wide range of gigs on an equally varied list of instruments, all in equal temperament. That's just simple job security. But for the next generation, wouldn't it be an obvious step in a music education curriculum to oblige teachers to introduce their students to the baroque repertoire by using the proper tool? Other instruments are approached that way. And not just as a 'Here's how it used to be done.' Seems obvious to me, but I know of a faculty of music not too far distant from where I live that has two trumpets of mine in a box. Furthermore, they've been in that box a long time, and I think opening it would be the equivalent of Howard Carter entering Tutankhamen's tomb. No change in behaviour happening there any time soon!

But here's a thought: when they're playing their trumpets in an ensemble with no other instruments, why shouldn't the musicians try going *au naturelle*? Personally, I think an 18th century trumpet ensemble playing with fingerholes looks downright ridiculous. And worse if they're dressed in period costumes. Come on, people! Just look at yourselves![6] Remember the old days (well, us old farts do; maybe you're too young) when people played stuff because they knew it was different, and they knew their audiences would be fascinated, intrigued, delighted? Live a little. Why not try some public education?

Changes in Cognition
This is why the myth of Henry VIII's motorcycle is so appealing. Its creation offers a change in cognition—the fabrication of a narrative to believe in—thus

assuaging the guilt of having to live a lie. But it just won't do anymore, will it? It's time to stop believing in historical fiction. I write the stuff, but I don't ever *believe* it. I think it's high time for all concerned to cut the rubbish and stop pretending, not just to themselves but to the public at large. No artist worth their salt needs to misrepresent their art, especially through the invention of a false narrative.

The Three Strategies

So, two out of the three strategies show some promise. (I exclude the firelighters.) With yet another generation of music students being introduced to the vented jobbie, I do tend to despair. A short while ago there was a video clip of a sweet little girl of perhaps eight years old, playing notes beautifully on a natural trumpet. For goodness sake, I said to myself, don't wreck her innocence. Or if you're going to give her a colander to blow into, at least don't teach her to tell lies about it. Perhaps, I dreamt, when she reaches the age when her handspan is large enough to reach the holes, she'll look her teachers right in the eye and ask them what planet they think they're from.

Wouldn't that be nice?

Going Forward

The title of this section is a poke at those people, politicians in particular, who use this phrase when they've put their brains in neutral. There is no other direction in which to go: while with baroque music we like to *look* backward, we can no more go in that direction of time than we can go sideways. So, going forward (by the immutable laws that govern the universe) this is the place where I shoot myself in the foot, blowing a hole in my entire plea for honesty, probity and ethical behaviour. It's this: from the point of view of those looking from the outside, we all know that not one concert-goer in a hundred *really* wonders about those holes. Or cares. That's why this hoax has gone on for as long as it has. It has got to the point where it has adherents who will stand up in public and repeat absolute falsehoods with a straight face. Each stage of the journey, from 'Hey, look at this, a trumpet with a hole' over 60 years ago, through decisions on pitch and temperament, paths of expediency, and the production of craftier and craftier inventions, have all led inevitably to this place. The *modus operandi* has been locked in tight by a concatenation of events, decisions and choices; the collective will to drive on this side of the road and no other is now irreversible. And, in truth, it's only old curmudgeons like me who give a damn, and it won't be long before you don't have to bother about me anymore either.

You win; I lose.

The musical powers-that-be have succeeded in rewriting history, and I hope they are proud of that accomplishment. Me? In their shoes, I would be downright ashamed, not of the distortion in historical performance—because that has been excusably driven by the exigencies of the commercial necessity for standardization—but by their collective efforts over the years to ensure that their audiences would come to believe their fabrication.

That is unconscionable.

Now, just to show you how naïve I was nearly 30 years ago, I'm going to make the tasteless *gaucherie* of quoting myself again:

> Perhaps before this decade has passed the whole controversy of the playability of the instrument and the willingness of the player will have been reassessed and the trumpet will finally take its place among all the other instruments of the Baroque orchestra whose teething problems are far in the past.[7]

Ha!

But that's only one half of the *Tale of Two Trumpets*, of course. Pull a chair up to the table, there's a delicious other half laid out for you, a banquet for the discerning baroque music lover. So, as a final note, let's salute again those I cited in my Dedication; the individuals who continue to hold the line, practicing the natural trumpet, contrary to the largely popular ventilated trend. To give readers a full idea of the devotion, trials and successes of these trumpeters, I can strongly recommend Julian Zimmermann's website, which covers the history, music and practice in great detail.[8] One can also view some excellent videos on-line, among which are Mr Zimmermann in a Telemann concerto for trumpet, two oboes and basso continuo;[9] and Jean-François Madeuf in a sonata by Heinrich Biber.[10] The instrument is played flawlessly and with great beauty.

Of course, there are places of education where compromises are considered unacceptable, and where students are taught the craft as it was, and as it now should be. But the trumpeters can't do it alone. They need to enlist the teamwork of the whole ensemble, which is what the word orchestra implies.[11] Happily, there are enlightened music directors who have always known that new and unappreciated aspects of the music are there to be discovered when it's done right. Graham Nicholson says it best:

> Throughout the first decade of this century, it has been possible to re-create this lost art, not by means of artifice and acoustic cunning but by the same hard work and desire for truth, the same tenacity and spirit of experiment that created the instrument and its musical repertory in the first place."[12]

Now, I think, we have come to the perfect place for His Majesty to put the brakes on and switch off his engine.

Notes

[1] http://www.tuftl.tufts.edu/musicengineering/research/cryo/cryo_paper_asa.pdf
[2] 'We'd better play well, or he'll invite the English!' It was a lovely irony, years later, to see the French appearing at the Royal Albert Hall and showing the English how to play their own Handel: https://www.youtube.com/watch?v=fNqJ8mED1VE
[3] A thing that is hoped or wished for but is, in fact, illusory or impossible to achieve.
[4] Festinger, Leon, *A Theory of Cognitive Dissonance* (Stanford: Stanford University Press, 1957)
[5] In the very first paragraph of his chapter on 'The Natural and Baroque Trumpet,' John Foster mentions the popular confusion between 'natural' and 'baroque' and considers it 'most important to make [the] distinction.' Although expressed in a technical publication, this is the kind of honesty that could well percolate into the public sphere of baroque music making. (*The Natural Trumpet and Other Related Instruments* (Cookaburra Music, 2010, p. 5.)
[6] I was at a medieval fayre once where there was this court jester tricked out in the usual Hollywood regalia—Harlequin weskit, pointy shoes, silly hat with bells—à la Danny Kaye. The wanker was playing a Japanese nickel-silver flute!
[7] Barclay *op cit* (1992) p. 175.
[8] https://naturtrompete.ch/en/643-2/
[9] https://www.youtube.com/watch?v=yjR4g1yClcM
[10] https://www.youtube.com/watch?v=dBA7FlUsFnk
[11] Ancient Greek ὀρχήστρα, the front of the stage where the chorus was located.
[12] Nicholson *op cit* (2010), p. 200.

Postamble

A word from our sponsors
or
Some blatant self-promotion

Robert Barclay

Making a Natural Trumpet
Herstellung einer Naturtrompete

This book is a graphic description of the International Trumpet-making Workshop, which has been in operation since 1994. Participants in this workshop make a natural trumpet based on a 17th century original using the materials, tools and techniques of the period. Every stage of the workshop is illustrated in over 70 colour photographs, and background information on the trumpet model chosen, the history of the workshop, and further references are also included. This book is a must-have for anyone, musician or not, who is interested in the history and construction of the natural trumpet and its performance today.

Dieses Buch ist eine Beschreibung des Internationalen Trompetenbau-Workshops, welcher 1994 begann. Teilnehmer des Workshops bauen eine Naturtrompete basierend auf einem Original des 17 Jahrhunderts unter Verwendung von Materialien, Werkzeugen und Techniken dieser Periode. Jeder Schritt des Workshops wird in über 70 Farbfotos illustriert. Es werden Hintergrundinformationen zum Trompetenmodell erläutert und die Geschichte des Workshops dargestellt. Referenzen über den Workshop sind ebenfalls enthalten. Dieses Buch ist ein Muss für jeden, Musiker oder nicht, der sich für die Geschichte und den Bau der Naturtrompete interessiert und ihre heutige Spielweise.

>Available from:
>www.loosecannonpress.com
>Or online as hard copy or e-book

Jacob the Trumpeter

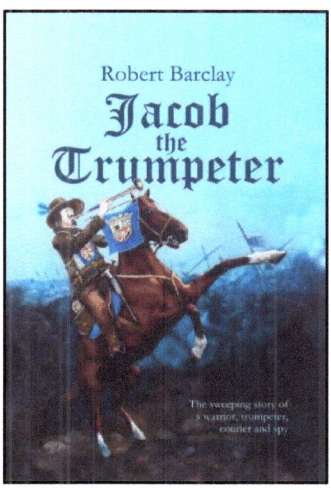

If you have enjoyed reading my last kick at the trumpet can, I am sure you will enjoy Jacob Hintze's tale, a sweeping saga set in 17th century Germany. Since he first heard a herald in the marketplace when he was ten years old, all Jacob has wanted to do is play the trumpet. Apprenticed to a German cavalry unit as a teenager, he is thrown into the horrors of the Thirty Years War. Employed as a courier and secret agent by his Duke, Jacob meets love, hatred, vengeance and betrayal as around him Europe tears itself to pieces. He plays his trumpet on the battlefield to send men to their deaths; he makes music in holy service to the glory of God. Jacob Hintze's life story is a stirring struggle in which music, war, espionage and the love of a good woman wrestle for his soul on a backdrop of bloody conflict and fragile peace. A rattlin' good yarn.

> Available from:
> www.loosecannonpress.com
> Or online as paperback or e-book

His Majesty's Grand Conceit

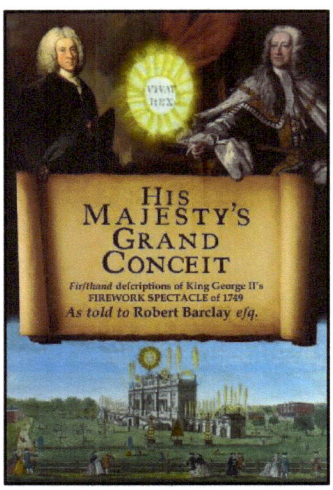

Here's something for the historical fiction afficionados. In 1748 a mighty edifice rose in the Green Park in London's west end, the launching pad for a grand firework to celebrate the Peace of Aix-la-Chapelle and Britannia's might! But what was King George II thinking when he decided to employ Frenchmen and Italians to undertake it? Did he believe the celebration of Peace meant peace between nations? And what of Mr London Town, still smarting from a peace that was none to his liking and benefitting him not at all? Enter John Montagu, a highly capable and well-connected diplomat, courtier and statesman, to take on the task of realizing His Majesty's grand conceit. From the first spade in the ground to the shattering conclusion, here is the story from ten characters, including George Frideric Handel, who witnessed and participated. And what a tortuous path the story takes.

>Available from:
>www.loosecannonpress.com
>Or online as paperback or e-book

The Birckholtz Trumpet of 1650

Jean-François Madeuf and Ensemble play music on copies of a trumpet by Wolfgang Birckholtz of Nürnberg, in concert with other instruments. The original trumpet, made in 1650, was discovered by Michael Münkwitz in a small church in eastern Germany, where it had been hanging since 1676, attached to a votive plaque commemorating trumpeter Jacob Hintze, who was killed in a duel. The CD features copies made in Herr Münkwitz's workshop using historical techniques. The original instrument is now in the collection of the Germanisches Nationalmuseum, and a copy of it hangs on the plaque in the church. For a historical recreation of Hintze's life see *Jacob the Trumpeter* (page 57).

>Available from:
>www.trompetenmacher.de/en/

Robert Barclay

Feedback
Corrections, Additions, Subtractions and Criticism

Modern technology gives us the great advantage of making changes easily. The print-on-demand process allows a new version of a text to be uploaded instantly and at very little cost. Gone are the days when an author had a pile of 10 boxes in the basement, each containing 100 books, every single one of which bore the same embarrassing and irreversible mistakes. (Well, maybe one the boxes was short a few copies, because you'd given a signed one to your dear old mum, and perhaps a few to your friends.)

Anyhow, here's your chance to make the second edition of this *minimum opus* so much better through the benefit of your wisdom. I can learn from my mistakes and can reproduce them exactly, but you have the valuable ability to help me mend my ways while there is still time. I would hate to head toward the final light with the thought that there was business left undone.

By the way, I promised this would be the last thing I would ever write on this topic, but I never said anything about further editions.

Contact me through:
www.loosecannonpress.com

Cliché Competition

All great writing involves the use of cliché, and this author's work is no exception. Spot all 25 clichés and the first entry received will win a copy of *Making a Natural Trumpet: Herstellung einer Naturtrompete*. Any entrants giving a higher number, if judged legitimate, will be awarded a copy of the CD, *The Birckholtz Trumpet of 1650*. First come, first served. So, hurry!

Apply here for a chance at your prize:
loosecannonpress@gmail.com

www.ingramcontent.com/pod-product-compliance
Lightning Source LLC
Chambersburg PA
CBHW042303150426
43196CB00005B/67